The Family

OPPOSING VIEWPOINTS®

Other Books of Related Interest

The Family

OPPOSING VIEWPOINTS®

Auriana Ojeda, *Book Editor*

Daniel Leone, *President*
Bonnie Szumski, *Publisher*
Scott Barbour, *Managing Editor*
Helen Cothran, *Senior Editor*

OPPOSING
VIEWPOINTS®
SERIES

GREENHAVEN
PRESS®

NEW ENGLAND INSTITUTE OF TECHNOLOGY
LIBRARY

THOMSON
───────★───────™
GALE

San Diego • Detroit • New York • San Francisco • Cleveland
New Haven, Conn. • Waterville, Maine • London • Munich

LIBRARY OF CONGRESS CATALOGING-IN-PUBLICATION DATA

The family / Auriana Ojeda, book editor.
    p. cm. — (Opposing viewpoints series)
Includes bibliographical references and index.
ISBN 0-7377-1228-7 (lib. : alk. paper) — ISBN 0-7377-1227-9 (pbk. : alk. paper)
    1. Family—United States. 2. Adoption—United States. 3. Family
services—United States. I. Ojeda, Auriana, 1977– . II. Opposing viewpoints series
(Unnumbered)
HQ536 .F33814 2003
306.85'0973—dc21   2002034726

Printed in the United States of America

> "Congress shall make no law...abridging the freedom of speech, or of the press."

First Amendment to the U.S. Constitution

The basic foundation of our democracy is the First Amendment guarantee of freedom of expression. The Opposing Viewpoints Series is dedicated to the concept of this basic freedom and the idea that it is more important to practice it than to enshrine it.

Contents

Why Consider
Opposing Viewpoints?

"The only way in which a human being can make some approach to knowing the whole of a subject is by hearing what can be said about it by persons of every variety of opinion and studying all modes in which it can be looked at by every character of mind. No wise man ever acquired his wisdom in any mode but this."

John Stuart Mill

In our media-intensive culture it is not difficult to find differing opinions. Thousands of newspapers and magazines and dozens of radio and television talk shows resound with differing points of view. The difficulty lies in deciding which opinion to agree with and which "experts" seem the most credible. The more inundated we become with differing opinions and claims, the more essential it is to hone critical reading and thinking skills to evaluate these ideas. Opposing Viewpoints books address this problem directly by presenting stimulating debates that can be used to enhance and teach these skills. The varied opinions contained in each book examine many different aspects of a single issue. While examining these conveniently edited opposing views, readers can develop critical thinking skills such as the ability to compare and contrast authors' credibility, facts, argumentation styles, use of persuasive techniques, and other stylistic tools. In short, the Opposing Viewpoints Series is an ideal way to attain the higher-level thinking and reading skills so essential in a culture of diverse and contradictory opinions.

In addition to providing a tool for critical thinking, Opposing Viewpoints books challenge readers to question their own strongly held opinions and assumptions. Most people form their opinions on the basis of upbringing, peer pressure, and personal, cultural, or professional bias. By reading carefully balanced opposing views, readers must directly confront new ideas as well as the opinions of those with whom they disagree. This is not to simplistically argue that everyone who reads opposing views will—or should—change his or her opinion. Instead, the series enhances readers' understanding of their own views by encouraging confrontation with opposing ideas. Careful examination of others' views can lead to the readers' understanding of the logical inconsistencies in their own opinions, perspective on why they hold an opinion, and the consideration of the possibility that their opinion requires further evaluation.

Evaluating Other Opinions

To ensure that this type of examination occurs, Opposing Viewpoints books present all types of opinions. Prominent spokespeople on different sides of each issue as well as well-known professionals from many disciplines challenge the reader. An additional goal of the series is to provide a forum for other, less known, or even unpopular viewpoints. The opinion of an ordinary person who has had to make the decision to cut off life support from a terminally ill relative, for example, may be just as valuable and provide just as much insight as a medical ethicist's professional opinion. The editors have two additional purposes in including these less known views. One, the editors encourage readers to respect others' opinions—even when not enhanced by professional credibility. It is only by reading or listening to and objectively evaluating others' ideas that one can determine whether they are worthy of consideration. Two, the inclusion of such viewpoints encourages the important critical thinking skill of objectively evaluating an author's credentials and bias. This evaluation will illuminate an author's reasons for taking a particular stance on an issue and will aid in readers' evaluation of the author's ideas.

It is our hope that these books will give readers a deeper understanding of the issues debated and an appreciation of the complexity of even seemingly simple issues when good and honest people disagree. This awareness is particularly important in a democratic society such as ours in which people enter into public debate to determine the common good. Those with whom one disagrees should not be regarded as enemies but rather as people whose views deserve careful examination and may shed light on one's own.

Thomas Jefferson once said that "difference of opinion leads to inquiry, and inquiry to truth." Jefferson, a broadly educated man, argued that "if a nation expects to be ignorant and free . . . it expects what never was and never will be." As individuals and as a nation, it is imperative that we consider the opinions of others and examine them with skill and discernment. The Opposing Viewpoints Series is intended to help readers achieve this goal.

David L. Bender and Bruno Leone,
Founders

Greenhaven Press anthologies primarily consist of previously published material taken from a variety of sources, including periodicals, books, scholarly journals, newspapers, government documents, and position papers from private and public organizations. These original sources are often edited for length and to ensure their accessibility for a young adult audience. The anthology editors also change the original titles of these works in order to clearly present the main thesis of each viewpoint and to explicitly indicate the opinion presented in the viewpoint. These alterations are made in consideration of both the reading and comprehension levels of a young adult audience. Every effort is made to ensure that Greenhaven Press accurately reflects the original intent of the authors included in this anthology.

Introduction

"Romantic love is a kind of spiritual breath each of us was raised on, hopes for, dreams of, and expects in our lives. Those of us who have it can scarcely imagine life without it, as if we'd suffocate for lack of oxygen."

—E.J. Graff

When asked why they got married, most people say that they fell in love. American society associates marriage with romantic love and lifelong companionship. For most of history, however, marriage was a contractual arrangement that had more to do with practicality than love. Marriage was the primary institution through which the rich exchanged property and the poor found their main work partner. However, in the nineteenth century, marriage changed dramatically from a practical arrangement to a satisfying personal relationship. The primary reason for this shift was that the Industrial Revolution enabled people to earn a living that was independent of their parents' or spouse's wealth. This freedom allowed people to choose husbands or wives based on factors other than wealth, such as attraction, affection, and compatibility. As stated by E.J. Graff in *What Is Marriage For?*, "Precisely because we can each make our own living, with or without our families of origin, with or without a spouse, we have vastly more choice in matters of the heart."

Prior to the eighteenth century, marriage was strictly a financial arrangement. The deal usually began with the youths' parents setting the size of the dowry and bride price. A dowry is a marriage gift from the bride's family to the groom's family, and the bride price is a gift from the groom's family to the bride's family. In most marriages, neither the bride nor the groom, particularly of the upper class, had much say in their parents' (or more specifically, their father's) choice of spouse. Kings might marry their daughters to foreign royalty and unite their kingdoms, nobles could marry their sons to nearby landowners and combine their lands, or destitute earls might regain their fortunes by marrying wealthy merchants' daughters. As stated by Graff,

"Your marriage choice was not simply your own. Your family and friends were your board of directors, experienced people with a direct stake in guiding you to a successfully concluded merger."

People of the lower classes exchanged dowries and bride prices too, but they often had to earn their own instead of relying on inherited wealth. Large fortunes, tracts of land, or titles were not at stake, so, by earning their own dowry, working class individuals had more, though not sole, choice of whom they married. Marriage among the lower classes was still regarded as a practical arrangement or contract, however, and people married individuals who could help them earn a living. For example, a farmer's wife was regarded as his business partner, and she contributed as much to the family's upkeep as he did. According to historian Olwen Hufton, "The farmer's wife generally tended livestock, particularly chickens and pigs. . . , grew vegetables, did dairy work, kept bees, preserved and pickled, helped prepare goods for sale and perhaps took them to market, [and] lent a hand at harvest and during haymaking." A lower class individual's total life income depended upon marriage, so it was practical to marry an able business partner who brought a substantial dowry or bride price to the marriage.

Social systems that centered on arranged marriages, dowries, and bride prices emphasized duty and obedience, and people had limited individual choice. Nearly everyone lived under the control of a master. A patriarchal family was a microcosm of the larger community and even larger kingdom. Children were subject to their parents just as peasants were subject to nobles and nobles were subject to royalty. Children were taught the value of obedience and duty and were even seen as their parents' property. As stated by historian Lawrence Stone, "Children are so much the goods, the possessions of their parents that they cannot, without a kind of theft, give themselves away without the allowance of those that have the right [to] them."

Choice was also limited because youths' daily lives differed little, if at all, from their parents' daily lives. Children typically took up the family business, married someone from their community, and rarely left their hometown. Children typically performed the same chores, ate the same food, and wore the same kinds of clothes as their parents. Adolescents' day-to-day lives were nearly identical to their parents', so it made sense to adopt their parents' traditions and methods for survival. Moreover, their parents often had survived famines, disease, or wars, so they knew how to overcome adversity. As stated by Graff, "For most people in most places, daily survival was achieved by obedience. . .: do as I did and you'll be more likely to live and thrive."

Around the eighteenth century, this system began to change, partly because the Industrial Revolution transformed society from an agriculture-based economy to a trade-based economy. New industries—textiles, mining, steam power, electrical power, transportation, and communication—sprang up all over the Western hemisphere. These industries powered a simultaneous growth in cities, as people flocked to urban areas in search of work. At the end of the seventeenth century, nearly 80 percent of people had lived in rural areas and earned their living from agriculture. By the end of the nineteenth century, nearly one-half of Europe's population resided in cities and made their living through trade.

The Industrial Revolution fostered a trade economy that helped free youths from their parents' control because it provided life options that had never been available before. For the first time, most people earned their own wealth and were not dependent upon their families to earn a living. They traveled to new towns, learned new trades, and, in the process, developed means of survival that deviated from those of their parents'. With these novel experiences, young people were devising new life philosophies that encouraged the pursuit of an independent, personally fulfilling lifestyle. As stated by Graff, "Children were slipping free from their parents' control—as more and more of us were becoming free to earn and therefore to travel, love, marry, and eventually think."

By 1850, the preindustrial system of marriage as a financial arrangement was nearly extinct in the West. In its place, the ideal of romantic love had triumphed. Of course, romantic love had existed before the nineteenth century, and some people may even have felt love for their spouses. However, the goal of marriage, prior to the nineteenth century, was not love but livelihood. After 1850, love became the guiding principle in choosing a spouse, and a loveless marriage was regarded with sadness and pity. People who married for reasons other than love were seen as mercenary and shallow. This romantic concept of marriage, with love as its essence and foundation, is what most contemporary Americans yearn for.

Social changes during the Industrial Revolution freed people to earn their own living, and in doing so, gave them the freedom to make their own decisions about marriage. Americans enjoy more individual wealth today than at any other time in history, and, in consequence, most Americans are free to enter into marriages of their choice that ideally fulfill their need for romantic love. *The Family: Opposing Viewpoints* examines marriage and other issues related to the American family in the following chapters: What Is the State of the Family? Is Conventional Marriage Necessary for Healthy Families? Does Adoption Benefit Families? How Can Families Best Be Supported? Examination of these issues provides readers with a broad understanding of the state of the American family today. To be sure, most Americans would agree that despite the many pressures threatening the marriage institution today, marriages based on genuine love have the greatest chance of success.

CHAPTER 1

What Is the State of the Family?

Chapter Preface

According to Peter Drucker, in his book *Post-Capitalist Society*, "Every few hundred years in western history . . . we cross a divide. Within a few short decades, society rearranges itself—its world view, its basic values, its social and political structures, its key institutions. Fifty years later, there is a new world. And the people born then cannot even imagine the world in which their grandparents lived and to which their own parents were born."

Changes in family structure over the last fifty years clearly demonstrate this world in transition. For example, the first-time marriage rate is at an all-time low, and over half of all first marriages are preceded by cohabitation (living with a romantic partner without being married). Indeed, since 1960, the number of cohabiting couples increased by nearly 1,000 percent. Moreover, the divorce rate has increased nearly sixfold since the 1960s. The percentage of children living with married biological parents fell from 73 percent in 1972 to 51.7 percent in 1998.

These figures reflect a decrease in traditional families—a married couple including a working father and a stay-at-home mother—and a rise in nontraditional families. Nontraditional families include single parent families, blended or step families, adopted or foster parent families, grandparent families, and same-sex parent families. In 1961, 38 percent of households consisted of married couples with children; in 1998, that figure fell to 26 percent. As stated by author Helen Wilkinson, "Diversity is king. . . . The umbilical cord between parenthood and marriage has been cut and, partly as a consequence, the nuclear family no longer defines the culture."

Wilkinson and others argue that society should accept and support nontraditional forms of family. They contend that the decline of the traditional family heralds the rebirth of new and dynamic family structures. Wilkinson states, "Periods of gestation are never easy, and no birth comes without labor pains. But as a society we are now faced with a clear choice. We can make the birth of tomorrow's family easier, less painful, even a source of delight. But to do that, we have to embrace changes and let go of the past. We have to broaden our horizons beyond the nuclear family and strive to see families as they really are. . . . We must learn to think in the future tense for the sake of the children."

There is a significant difference between the structure of most families fifty years ago and the structure of most families today. Understandably, such changes can produce stresses and strains in a society and give rise to controversy. The authors in the following chapter discuss the state of the American family and debate whether the many changes that have occurred have been beneficial.

1

"All too often a center of dysfunction, [the family] has become one with the heartless world that surrounds it."

Traditional Families Are Declining

Barbara LeBey

In the following viewpoint, Barbara LeBey argues that the pursuit of personal satisfaction that originated in the 1960s had many positive outcomes but also led to four factors that fractured the traditional family: the sexual revolution, women's liberation, divorce, and increased mobility. LeBey maintains that the sexual revolution and the women's liberation movement freed women to pursue education and career goals, but in doing so the movements changed traditional notions of motherhood and family that put children first. Moreover, marriage changed from a necessity to a choice, and attitudes toward divorce became more lenient. Finally, technological innovations in transportation and telecommunications, and corporate relocation, scattered family members across the world. LeBey is the author of *Family Estrangements: How They Begin, How to Mend Them, How to Cope with Them*.

As you read, consider the following questions:
1. According to the author, how did women benefit from increased career and job opportunities?
2. What does the author cite as the primary reason for Americans relocating?
3. What are three trends that result from disconnected nuclear families, according to the author?

Barbara LeBey, "American Families Are Drifting Apart," *USA Today*, Vol. 130, September 2001, pp. 20–22. Copyright © 2001 by Society for the Advancement of Education. Reproduced with permission.

A variety of reasons—from petty grievances to deep-seated prejudices, misunderstandings to all-out conflicts, jealousies, sibling rivalry, inheritance feuds, family business disputes, and homosexual outings—are cause for families to grow apart. Family estrangements are becoming more numerous, more intense, and more hurtful. When I speak to groups on the subject, I always ask: Who has or had an estrangement or knows someone who does? Almost every hand in the room goes up. Sisters aren't speaking to each other since one of them took the silver when Mom died. Two brothers rarely visit because their wives don't like each other. A son alienates himself from his family when he marries a woman who wants to believe that he sprung from the earth. Because Mom is the travel agent for guilt trips, her daughter avoids contact with her. A family banishes a daughter for marrying outside her race or religion. A son eradicates a divorced father when he reveals his homosexuality. And so it goes.

The Family Is Changing

The nation is facing a rapidly changing family relationship landscape. Every assumption made about the family structure has been challenged, from the outer boundaries of single mothers raising out-of-wedlock children to gay couples having or adopting children to grandparents raising their grandchildren. If the so-called traditional family is having trouble maintaining harmony, imagine what problems can and do arise in less-conventional situations. Fault lines in Americans' family structure were widening throughout the last 40 years of the 20th century. The cracks became evident in the mid 1970s when the divorce rate doubled. According to a 1999 Rutgers University study, divorce has risen 30% since 1970; the marriage rate has fallen faster; and just 38% of Americans consider themselves happy in their married state, a drop from 53% 25 years ago. Today, 51% of all marriages end in divorce.

How Americans managed to alter their concept of marriage and family so profoundly during those four decades is the subject of much scholarly investigation and academic debate. In a May 2000, *New York Times Magazine* article titled

"The Pursuit of Autonomy," the writer maintains that "the family is no longer a haven; all too often a center of dysfunction, it has become one with the heartless world that surrounds it." Unlike the past, the job that fits you in your 20s is not the job or career you'll likely have in your 40s. This is now true of marriage as well—the spouse you had in your 20s may not be the one you will have after you've gone through your midlife crisis.

In the 1960s, four main societal changes occurred that have had an enormous impact on the traditional family structure. The sexual revolution, women's liberation movement, states' relaxation of divorce laws, and mobility of American families have converged to foster family alienation, exacerbate old family rifts, and create new ones. It must be emphasized, however, that many of these changes had positive outcomes. The nation experienced a strengthened social conscience, women's rights, constraints on going to war, and a growing tolerance for diversity, but society also paid a price.

The 1960s perpetuated the notion that we are first and foremost entitled to happiness and fulfillment. It's positively unAmerican not to seek it! This idea goes back to that early period of our history when Thomas Jefferson dropped the final term from British philosopher John Locke's definition of human rights—"life, liberty, and . . . property"—and replaced it with what would become the slogan of our new nation: "the pursuit of happiness." In the words of author Gail Sheehy, the 1960s generation "expressed their collective personality as idealistic, narcissistic, anti-establishment, hairy, horny and preferably high."

Any relationship that was failing to deliver happiness was being tossed out like an empty beer can, including spousal ones. For at least 20 years, the pharmaceutical industry has learned how to cash in on the American obsession with feeling good by hyping mood drugs to rewire the brain circuitry for happiness through the elimination of sadness and depression.

Young people fled from the confines of family, whose members were frantic, worrying about exactly where their adult children were and what they were doing. There were probably more estrangements between parents and adult children during the 1960s and early 1970s than ever before.

Women's Liberation

In the wake of the civil rights movement and President Lyndon Johnson's Great Society came the women's liberation movement, and what a flashy role it played in changing perceptions about the family structure. Women who graduated from college in the late 1960s and early 1970s were living in a time when they could establish and assert their independent identities. In Atlanta, Emory Law School's 1968 graduating class had six women in it, the largest number ever to that point, and all six were in the top 10%, including the number-one graduate. In that same period, many all-male colleges opened their doors to women for the first time. No one could doubt the message singer Helen Reddy proclaimed: "I am woman, hear me roar." For all the self-indulgence of the "hippie" generation, there was an intense awakening in young people of a recognition that civil rights must mean equal rights for everyone in our society, and that has to include women.

Full equality was the battle cry of every minority, a status that women claimed despite their majority position. As they had once marched for the right to vote, women began marching for sexual equality and the same broad range of career and job opportunities that were always available to men. Financial independence gave women the freedom to walk away from unhappy marriages. This was a dramatic departure from the puritanical sense of duty that had been woven into the American fabric since the birth of this nation.

For all the good that came out of this movement, though, it also changed forever traditional notions of marriage, motherhood, and family unity, as well as that overwhelming sense of children first. Even in the most conservative young families, wives were letting their husbands know that they were going back to work or back to school. Many women had to return to work either because there was a need for two incomes to maintain a moderate standard of living or because they were divorced and forced to support their offspring on their own. "Don't ask, don't tell" day-care centers proliferated where overworked, undertrained staff, and two-income yuppie parents, ignored the children's emotional needs—all in the name of equality and to enable women to reclaim their identities. Some might say these were the parents who ran away from home.

Many states began to approve legislation that allowed no-fault divorce, eliminating the need to lay blame on spouses or stage adulterous scenes in sleazy motels to provide evidence for states that demanded such evidence for divorces. The legal system established procedures for easily dissolving marriages, dividing property, and sharing responsibility for the children. There were even do-it-yourself divorce manuals on bookstore shelves. Marriage had become a choice rather than a necessity, a one-dimensional status sustained almost exclusively by emotional satisfaction and not worth maintaining in its absence. Attitudes about divorce were becoming more lenient, so much so that the nation finally elected its first divorced president in 1980—Ronald Reagan. . . .

Family Mobility

The fourth change, and certainly one of the most pivotal, was the increased mobility of families that occurred during those four decades. Family members were no longer living in close proximity to one another. The organization man moved to wherever he could advance more quickly up the corporate ladder. College graduates took the best job offer, even if it was 3,000 miles away from where they grew up and where their family still lived.

Some were getting out of small towns for new vistas, new adventures, and new job opportunities. Others were fleeing the overcrowded dirty cities in search of cleaner air, a more reasonable cost of living, and retirement communities in snow-free, warmer, more scenic locations. Moving from company to company had begun, reaching what is now a crescendo of job-hopping. Many young people chose to marry someone who lived in a different location, so family ties were geographically severed for indeterminate periods of time, sometimes forever.

According to Lynn H. Dennis' *Corporate Relocation Takes Its Toll on Society*, during the 10 years from 1989 to 1999, more than 5,000,000 families were relocated one or more times by their employers. In addition to employer-directed moves, one out of five Americans relocated at least once, not for exciting adventure, but for economic advancement and/or a safer place to raise children. From March 1996, to March 1997, 42,000,000 Americans, or 16% of the population, packed up and moved from where they were living to another location. That is a striking statistic. Six million of these people moved from one region of the country to another, and young adults aged 20 to 29 were the most mobile, making up 32% of the moves during that year. This disbursement of nuclear families throughout the country disconnected them from parents, brothers, sisters, grandparents, aunts, uncles, and cousins—the extended family and all its adhesive qualities.

The Modern Family Is Here to Stay

Overall, the shift from traditional to modern family structures and values is likely to continue. This is especially true of the shift to dual-earner couples and egalitarian gender roles, although the impetus towards single-parent families is less certain. The divorce rate has stabilized, albeit at a high level, and non-marital births have stopped rising and may be falling. These factors will tend to curb the continued growth of single-parent families, although they are unlikely to lead to their decline.

Few areas of society have changed as much as the family has over the last generation. Collectively the alterations mark the replacement of traditional family types and family values with the emerging, modern family types and a new set of family values.

As [philosopher] Meng-tzu has noted, "The root of the state is the family," and the ongoing transplantation of the family has uprooted society in general. Some changes have been good, others bad, and still others both good and bad. But given the breadth and depth of changes in family life, the changes both for the better and the worse have been disruptive. Society has had to readjust to continually evolving structures and new attitudes. It is through this process of structural and value change and adaptation to these changes that the modern, 21st century family is emerging.

Tom Smith, *The Public Perspective*, January/February 2001.

Today, with cell phones, computers, faxes, and the Internet, the office can be anywhere, including in the home. Therefore, we can live anywhere we want to. If that is the case, why aren't more people choosing to live in the cities or towns where they grew up? There's no definitive answer. Except for the praise heaped on "family values," staying close to family no longer plays a meaningful role in choosing where we reside. . . .

The Extended Family Is Vital

Our culture tends to focus on the individual, or, at most, on the nuclear family, downplaying the benefits of extended families, though their role is vital in shaping our lives. The notion of "moving on" whenever problems arise has been a time-honored American concept. Too many people would rather cast aside some family member than iron out the situation and keep the relationship alive. If we don't get along with our father or if our mother doesn't like our choice of mate or our way of life, we just move away and see the family once or twice a year. After we're married, with children in school, and with both parents working, visits become even more difficult. If the family visits are that infrequent, why bother at all? Some children grow up barely knowing any of their relatives. Contact ceases; rifts don't resolve; and divisiveness often germinates into a full-blown estrangement.

In an odd sort of way, the more financially independent people become, the more families scatter and grow apart. It's not a cause, but it is a facilitator. Tolerance levels decrease as financial means increase. Just think how much more we tolerate from our families when they are providing financial support. Look at the divorced wife who depends on her family for money to supplement alimony and child support, the student whose parents are paying all college expenses, or the brother who borrows family money to save his business.

Recently, a well-known actress being interviewed in a popular magazine was asked, if there was one thing she could change in her family, what would it be? Her answer was simple: "That we could all live in the same city." She understood the importance of being near loved ones and how, even in a harmonious family, geographical distance often leads to emotional disconnectedness. When relatives are regularly in each other's company, they will usually make a greater effort to get along. Even when there is dissension among family members, they are more likely to work it out, either on their own or because another relative has intervened to calm the troubled waters. When rifts occur, relatives often need a real jolt to perform an act of forgiveness. Forgiving a family member can be the hardest thing to do, probably because the emotional bonds are so much deeper and usually go all the way back to childhood. Could it be that blood is a thicker medium in which to hold a grudge?

Keep It Together

With today's families scattered all over the country, the matriarch or patriarch of the extended family is far less able to keep his or her kin united, caring, and supportive of one another. In these disconnected nuclear families, certain trends—workaholism, alcoholism, depression, severe stress, isolation, escapism, and a push toward continuous supervised activity for children—are routinely observed. What happened to that family day of rest and togetherness? We should mourn its absence.

For the widely dispersed baby boomers with more financial means than any prior generation, commitment, intimacy, and family togetherness have never been high on their list of priorities. How many times have you heard of family members trying to maintain a relationship with a relative via e-mail and answering machines? One young man now sends his Mother's Day greeting by leaving a message for his mom on his answering machine. When she calls to scold him for forgetting to call her, she'll get a few sweet words wishing her a happy Mother's Day and his apology for being too busy to call or send a card! His sister can expect the same kind of greeting for her birthday, but only if she bothers to call to find out why her brother hadn't contacted her.

Right now, and probably for the foreseeable future, we will be searching for answers to the burgeoning problems we unwittingly created by these societal changes, but don't be unduly pessimistic. Those who have studied and understood the American psyche are far more optimistic. The 19th-century French historian and philosopher Alexis de Tocqueville once said of Americans, "No natural boundary seems to be set to the effort of Americans, and in their eyes what is not yet done, is only what they have not yet attempted to do." Some day, I hope this mindset will apply not to political rhetoric on family values, but to bringing families back together again.

"After more than three decades of relentless advance, the family structure revolution in the U.S. may be over."

The Decline of Traditional Families May Be Over

David Blankenhorn

In the following viewpoint, David Blankenhorn argues that statistics suggesting that the traditional family is declining are inaccurate. He contends that the number of traditional families in America declined to an all-time low in 1997, but claims that the number has since stabilized. Blankenhorn maintains that these figures suggest an end to the family structure revolution, which heralds a positive change for American families and society. Blankenhorn is the founder and president of the Institute for American Values, an organization dedicated to promoting marriage and family.

As you read, consider the following questions:
1. Why does the author blame the confusion over family statistics on the Census Bureau?
2. According to Blankenhorn, what was the primary basis for the "decline stories" in May 2001?
3. What causes does the author attribute to the shift in family decline?

David Blankenhorn, "The Reappearing Nuclear Family," *First Things*, January 2002, pp. 20–23.

As if it didn't have enough to fret about, the two-parent American family got taken for quite a ride in 2001. First, in April the Census Bureau dramatically reported that the "nuclear family" was "rebounding." The page-one story in *USA Today* announced: "The traditional nuclear family—a married mom and dad living with their biological children—is making a comeback, according to a Census report released today. The proportion of the nation's children living with both biological parents jumped from 51 percent in 1991 to 56 percent . . . in 1996." On ABC World News Tonight, Peter Jennings declared: "The Census Bureau said today that the number of children who live with both their parents increased during the 1990s." Scores of news organizations around the country reported the same happy story.

But in May, the story reversed itself. Journalists across the country began to report that "nuclear families" now constitute less than 25 percent of all U.S. households. An editorial in the *New York Post* announced that "the American nuclear family" was now "up there with the Pacific salmon as an endangered species." A *Newsweek* cover story on unmarried mothers ("the new faces of America's family album") explained at length how the "traditional family" was "fading fast." Dr. James Dobson, the radio personality and president of Focus on the Family, an influential Christian pro-family organization, said that the "alarming" Census Bureau figures revealed "just how dire the situation has become," as "the family is unraveling at a faster pace than ever." The *New York Times* took a sunnier view. Following up on its page-one news story ("Number of Nuclear Families Drops as 1-Parent Families Rise"), the *Times* editorial board urged its readers not to worry about the decline, since "the nuclear family is not the only kind of family or even the only healthy kind of family."

Well, now. Is it possible for the nuclear family to be simultaneously "making a comeback" and "fading fast"? Of course not. So which is true? Amazingly enough, the answer is neither. What is actually happening to U.S. family structure is quite different from the news conveyed by either cycle of stories.

While the Census Bureau has been quick to blame the media for the confusion, the fault lies primarily with the Bureau. For mysterious reasons, the Census Bureau chose in the fine print of its April 2001 report to define a "traditional nuclear family" as a household consisting of two biological parents, their minor children, and no one else. That is, a household that includes grandparents is not "traditional." A household that includes boarders, or a foster child, is not "traditional." Moreover, during the 1990s, for reasons that have almost nothing to do with the core issue—which is how many U.S. children are growing up in households with two married parents—three-generation and large or complex households with children declined slightly as a proportion of all households with children.

That little curio of a demographic fact—that tangent of a tangent—was the entire basis of the Census Bureau's April "rebound" report. No evidence presented in that report justifies the assertion that the proportion of children living with both biological parents rose during the early- and mid-1990s. And to add injury to insult, the obscurantist definition of "traditional" means that the Census Bureau, while allegedly describing a nuclear family "rebound," actually underreported the proportion of U.S. children living with two married parents. The Census Bureau report puts the figure at 56 percent for 1996. But my own research, subsequently confirmed by other researchers and the Census Bureau itself, shows that the actual figure for 1996 is 64 percent.

As for May 2001's precipitous drop in optimism, it can be traced to further manipulation of definitions on the part of journalists with no helpful guidance and arguably even some complicity from the Census Bureau. This time, using a data table released in mid-May with much fanfare by the Census Bureau, journalism chose to measure married-couple-with-children families not as a proportion of all families (two or more persons living together related by blood, marriage, or adoption), but instead as a proportion of all households. Grandma living on her own is a household. College roommates sharing an apartment are a household. The number of non-family households in the U.S. has been growing steadily for many decades for multiple reasons (including longer life spans and greater affluence), most of which have little to do with the state of marriage and child rearing. Indeed, marriedswith-children were a distinct minority of all U.S. households even in the 1950s. That's why most scholars agree that the best way to measure the prevalence of a family phenomenon such as marriage is to place it in the context of family households; throwing in non-family households is like mixing apples and oranges. This piece of confusion was the primary basis for the "decline" stories that received so much attention in May 2001.

Getting the Facts

Families consisting of a married couple with children under age 18 have not been in a majority since 1967. While the proportion of such families has declined dramatically in the intervening years, the rate of decline has recently been leveling off, according to Census Bureau officials.

- Married couples with minor children accounted for 35.7 percent of families in 1997—down from 50.1 percent in 1967 and 36.3 percent in 1993.

- As a proportion of all households, married-couple households with children declined from 40 percent to 26 percent between 1970 and 1990.

- The percentage of single-parent families in the U.S. doubled between 1970 and 1990—from 6 percent to 12 percent of all families and from 11 percent to 24 percent of all households.

- From 1990 to 1997, the percentage of single-parent families edged up by less than 2 points.

The divorce rate per 1,000 people was 4.1 in 1995—down from 4.7 in 1990 and 5.0 in 1985.

National Center for Policy Analysis, May 1998.

This episode is a distressing example of irresponsibility by a public agency charged with collecting and reporting data on how we live. Even at this late date, it is impossible for scholars to get accurate trend-line data from the Census Bureau on the proportion of U.S. children living with their two biological married parents. In June 2001, nine senior family scholars, led by Norval Glenn of the University of Texas and Linda Waite of the University of Chicago, wrote a public letter to the Census Bureau asking it to disentangle the definitions and report this basic information. The Census Bureau politely declined. For the time being, at least, accurate information about this trend will have to come from elsewhere.

Independent Data

Which brings us to the truly good news. A series of recent reports from independent scholars, plus largely unpublished data from the 2000 Census, all suggest that the trend of family fragmentation that many analysts had assumed to be unstoppable suddenly stopped in its tracks around 1996.

What we are seeing is not (at least not yet) a "rebound." But it's certainly not a "decline." To be conservative, let's call it a cessation, a significant pause. But let's say it more optimistically: after more than three decades of relentless advance, the family structure revolution in the U.S. may be over.

Here are the basic numbers. The proportion of all U.S. families with children under age eighteen that are headed by married couples reached an all-time low in the mid 1990s— about 72.9 percent in 1996 and 72.4 percent in 1997—but has since stabilized. The figure for 2000 is 73 percent. Similarly, the proportion of all U.S. children living in two-parent homes reached an all-time low in the mid-1990s, but since then has stabilized as well. In fact, the proportion of children in two-parent homes increased slightly from 68 percent in 1999 to 69.1 percent in 2000.

Looking only at white, non-Hispanic children, a study by Allan Dupree and Wendell Primus finds that the proportion of these children living with two married parents stopped its downward descent during the late 1990s, and even increased modestly from 1999 to 2000, rising from 77.3 to 78.2 percent. Another study from the Urban Institute finds that, among all U.S. children, the proportion living with their two biological or adoptive parents increased by 1.2 percent from 1997 to 1999, while during the same period the proportion living in stepfamilies (or blended families) decreased by 0.1 percentage points and the proportion living in single-parent homes decreased by two percentage points. (The study finds that in 1999 about 64 percent of all U.S. children lived with their two biological or adoptive parents, while about 25 percent lived with one parent and about 8 percent lived in a step or blended family.) Among low-income children, the decline in the proportion living in single-parent homes was even more pronounced, dropping from 44 percent in 1997 to 41 percent in 1999.

And, perhaps most encouraging, from 1995 to 2000 the proportion of African-American children living in two-parent, married-couple homes rose from 34.8 to 38.9 percent, a significant increase in just five years, representing the clear cessation and even reversal of the long-term shift toward black family fragmentation.

Reading Between the Lines

What has caused this shift? No one knows for sure, but we can make some plausible guesses. The roaring economy probably had little or nothing to do with it, since all previous economic booms since 1970 have coincided with growing family fragmentation, not reintegration. On the other hand, federal and state welfare reforms dating from the mid-1990s, which dramatically restructured and in some instances eliminated what had previously been guaranteed economic supports for unmarried mothers, have almost certainly played a role. As the above-cited data suggest, post-1995 family structure changes have been most dramatic among low-income families.

More generally, on the core social question of whether family fragmentation is a bad thing or a not-so-bad thing, a steady shift in popular and (especially) elite opinion took place over the course of the 1990s. Denial and happy talk about the consequences of nuclear family decline became decidedly less widespread; concern and even alarm became much more common. As a society we changed our minds, and as a result we changed some of our laws. And now, it seems, we are beginning to change some of our personal behavior. This is very encouraging news.

It is now clear that those who have long and loudly insisted that nothing can be done to stop the trend of family fragmentation are wrong. Remember all their cliches? We have to be realistic, they opined. The "family diversity" trend is irreversible. We can't put the toothpaste back in the tube. We shouldn't fall into the "nostalgia trap." We can't go back to "Ozzie and Harriet." Well, the next time someone tells you that, just smile and show him the new numbers. Positive change in U.S. family structure is not only desirable and possible. It is already occurring. Today our main challenge is no longer to reverse a trend toward disintegration, but to intensify the nascent trend toward reintegration.

"How and when can it be right for mothers and fathers to cause brutal pain to their children?"

Divorce Harms Children

Maggie Gallagher

In the following viewpoint, Maggie Gallagher challenges E. Mavis Hetherington's book *For Better or Worse: Divorce Reconsidered*, which contends that most children of divorced parents do not suffer devastating consequences later in life. Gallagher argues that Hetherington trivializes many of the severe effects of divorce on children, such as poor relationships with their fathers, engaging in premature sex, and teenage pregnancy. According to Gallagher, divorce inflicts intense pain on children, and parents should find a less damaging path to personal fulfillment. Gallagher is an affiliate scholar at the Institute for American Values in New York.

As you read, consider the following questions:

1. According to the author, what are the different reasons men and women give for divorcing?
2. What factor later improved divorced people's lives, as stated by Gallagher?
3. What does the author contend is the potential danger raised by Hetherington's research?

Maggie Gallagher, "Third Thoughts on Divorce," *National Review*, Vol. 54, March 25, 2002, p. 50. Copyright © 2002 by *National Review*. Reproduced with permission.

E. Mavis Hetherington is one of the nation's most re-spected research psychologists. Her book *For Better or Worse: Divorce Reconsidered*, (with writer John Kelly) has been marketed as a rebuttal to divorce critics, who—she be-lieves—have overestimated the negative effects of divorce and downplayed its benefits.

All the headlines have gone to Hetherington's bottom line: The majority of children of divorce, she reassures wor-ried parents, are functioning in the normal range 20 years later: "Most were successfully going about the chief tasks of young adulthood: establishing careers, creating intimate re-lationships, building meaningful lives."

But E. Mavis Hetherington is too good a scholar to have 20 years of research summed up in sound bites. This book is a report for lay readers on three different—and impor-tant—long-running studies designed to assess the effects of divorce. The studies ultimately involved 1,400 families; in other words, when it comes to the case against the case against divorce, this is as good as it gets. How good is that?

Adults and Divorce

Adults, first. Men and women divorced for different reasons, says Hetherington. Women complained about lack of inti-macy and affection; men complained about lack of sex and overly critical wives. Infidelity, abuse, and alcoholism were present, but in a minority of divorces.

Adults choose to divorce, then, not mostly to escape from violent hellholes, but because they are lonely, bored, de-pressed, dissatisfied. How often does divorce deliver on its seductive promise of a better life? Hetherington's sample consists mostly of white, middle-class, and relatively well-educated men and women. Yet even among this advantaged group, the answer is: Surprisingly seldom.

Hetherington judges that 20 years after a divorce, only about 20 percent of divorced individuals (most of them women) were Enhancers, whose lives were improved by the divorce. Another 10 percent became what Hetherington calls Competent Loners—whether divorce improved their lives is not clear. For about 40 percent, divorce was a tumult that made no difference: "Different partners, different marriages, but usually the same problems." The remaining 30 percent were in various stages of just plain miserable: Hetherington uses words like "desperately unhappy," "empty, pointless," "clinically depressed," "joyless," and "embittered" to describe how they felt about their lives.

Casual sex had a particularly negative effect on divorced women, notes Hetherington. The seven suicides she observed were all women and all triggered (she tells us) by casual sex. Men got bored with casual sex, too, but it took them two years, on average. (The ennui of meaningless sex eventually drove many a man to remarriage, but never to suicide.)

How good, then, is divorce for adults? Hetherington's work is peppered with data that are far from reassuring. Sentences like this, for example: "Behaviors like Peeping Tomism and harassing birds [girls] are worrisome, but they are also fairly normal in the first year after a divorce, as are erratic mood swings, vulnerability to psychological disorders and physical illness, and doubts about the decision to leave." Those who have entered the wacky world where Peeping Toms and bird assaults [assaults on girls] are fairly normal will no doubt be relieved to know there is a light at the end of the tunnel; the rest of us may be forgiven for thinking that jumping down that particular black hole sounds even less fun than one imagined.

Back to the Altar

What about the divorced people who were better off in the long run—what made the difference for them? The answer, ironically, is marriage. Hetherington found that "people in long-lasting, gratifying first and second marriages were better off economically, and had the lowest rates of depression, substance abuse, conduct disorders, health complaints, and visits to the doctor"—along with a more satisfying sex life.

Hetherington's study thus confirms the research of others on the critical importance of a good-enough marriage to adult well-being. But something about contemporary mores is seriously undermining the road to a good marriage. Only one-third of the grown children Hetherington studied (from intact and disrupted families) who were in the first seven years of marriage were very happily married, compared to over half of their parents at that stage; 38 percent reported facing a serious marital problem, compared to 20 percent of their parents at the same juncture. A good marriage is as important as it ever was, but apparently younger Americans are finding it harder and harder to achieve.

Children and Divorce

That's the upshot of Hetherington's study insofar as it concerns adults. But what about the kids? Should parents contemplating divorce relax?

'Blast. I forgot to ask for a receipt.'

Caz. © 1996 by *The Spectator*. Reprinted with permission.

On this issue, the results reported in *For Better or for Worse* are consistent with a large and growing social-science literature: Even among advantaged, middle-class white children, divorce doubles the risk that 20 years later the grown children will experience serious social, emotional, and/or psychological dysfunction. "Twenty-five percent of youths from divorced families in comparison to 10 percent from nondivorced families did have serious social, emotional, or psychological problems." Money didn't matter: Even when family incomes were similar, children from disrupted homes had more long-term dysfunction.

Three-quarters of children of divorce do function normally; does that mean the glass is only one-quarter empty? It is important to recognize the limitations inherent in the definition of damage Hetherington uses. Many children who are functioning in the normal range psychologically may be suffering in other ways. A child who does not go to a good college because her parents divorced is functioning in the normal range, for example. The 35 percent of girls in remarried homes who started menstruating before age 12 (compared to 18 percent of girls from intact homes) are certainly functioning normally. The increased risk of premature sex, sexually transmitted diseases, and teen pregnancy in children of divorce is mentioned by Hetherington, but only in passing.

Children of divorce in this study also had roughly double the divorce rate of children from low-conflict intact families, and a higher divorce risk even than children raised in unhappy marriages. Why? A lower commitment to marital permanence and fewer relationship skills, says Hetherington. Seventy percent of children of divorce who married had relatively permissive views of divorce, compared to 40 percent of spouses from intact families. Their best chance of marital success was to marry a child from an intact family.

One of the most consistent effects of divorce, even in white middle-class kids, was estrangement from the father. Very few of the highly educated and successful divorced men figured out how to be effective fathers outside of marriage. Twenty years later, about two-thirds of boys and three-quarters of girls had poor relationships with their fathers—compared to 30 percent of children from intact marriages.

Permanent Damage

The most poignant moment in the book is when Hetherington admits that "at the end of my study, a fair number of my adult children of divorce described themselves as permanently 'scarred.' But objective assessments of these 'victims' told a different story." What counts as damage has to be on

Professor Hetherington's checklist of dysfunctions defined by answers to multiple-choice questionnaires. The advantage, of course, is that these kinds of assessments are less likely to be influenced by the investigator's bias; but the equally obvious disadvantage is an enormous loss of sensitivity. When children of divorce try to tell Hetherington their own stories of more subtle, lingering emotional difficulties, she dismisses these as "self-fulfilling prophecy." If you have a job and a girlfriend, but you do not have your dad, does that count as damage? Not in Hetherington's book: You are functioning in the normal range, end of story.

Why would a top scholar such as Hetherington, whose own work recapitulates and confirms a growing consensus on the potential long-term negative effects of divorce, choose to minimize these effects in presenting her research to the public? Partly it is because she has a genuine admiration and respect for the personal growth divorce sometimes prompts, especially in women: Divorce winners do exist, most of them women who rise to meet and beat the considerable challenges divorce poses for mothers. Partly it is because Hetherington has defined down the damage caused by divorce, so that it includes only those consequences that can be categorized as social-science pathologies.

Certainly children of divorce need to know they are not damaged goods; human beings can rise above their circumstances. And certainly men and women who are already divorced need good advice on how to minimize the damage and maximize their opportunities. But the potential danger stemming from Hetherington's well-meaning message of encouragement is what it may convey to parents: Go ahead and divorce, your kids will do fine.

For concerned parents contemplating divorce, the news that 20 years later one-fourth of kids are seriously dysfunctional surely cannot be treated as good news. In no other context would responsible parents say, "Gee, only a one out of four chance I will permanently damage my child? Go for it!"

Parental Selfishness

But by framing the data in these terms, Hetherington raises an even deeper question: How much pain are parents entitled to inflict on their children, simply because their children may rise above it and avoid long-term psychological dysfunction? Like scholar Judith Wallerstein before her, Hetherington finds that even when divorce does not result in long-term damage, it is "usually brutally painful . . . To the boys and girls in my research divorce seemed cataclysmic and inexplicable. How could a child feel safe in a world where adults had suddenly become untrustworthy?"

One of Hetherington's success stories is a woman named Bethany. As an adult, she is doing extremely well, thanks to her mother's heroic parenting. I certainly do not blame her mother for choosing divorce—her husband's repeated infidelities were one proximate cause. And yet this is what divorce meant for Bethany: "The previously placid Bethany also would fly into rages, hitting and biting her mother, whom she blamed for the separation. In her distress, she began to wet the bed again, had night terrors, and would wake crying or crawl into bed with [her mother] three or four times a night. Bethany later said, 'I had to keep checking to see if Mom was there. If Dad could leave, why couldn't she?'"

The larger questions raised by these emotional realities of divorce are not, ultimately, scholarly ones. How and when can it be right for mothers and fathers to cause brutal pain to their children? If the human spirit is indeed resilient, can't enterprising adults perhaps find some other path to personal growth? How much are our ideas about the relative harmlessness of divorce undermining our ability to build the lasting love we crave?

| "Conflict, rather than separation itself, is
bad for children."

Divorce Need Not Harm Children

Suzanne Moore

According to Suzanne Moore, children suffer more from conflict within the home than from divorce. She argues that most of the problems that observers associate with divorce in reality stem from the poverty experienced by many single mothers and their children. She concludes that in order to protect children, society must effectively address poverty, and couples must learn to divorce in a way that minimizes conflict. Moore is a contributor to the *Independent*, a London-based newspaper.

As you read, consider the following questions:
1. According to Moore, what is the liberal view of divorce?
2. What does the author consider a "good" divorce?
3. What do parents hope to create with step-families, as stated by the author?

Everyone knows what is bad for children these days. Artificial additives, Teletubby overload and, of course, divorce. The children of divorcing parents will be aggressive, withdrawn and anxious. They may suffer low self-esteem, wet the bed, take drugs and many years later end up reproducing such misery by failing to sustain long-term relationships. Fathers lose contact with children, mothers become poorer, and boys especially suffer.

Sifting Through Statistics

If all of this, or indeed any of it, is true, then we need to worry, as already one in five children experiences the separation of their parents. To judge by recent rates of divorce, four in ten new marriages will not be till death us do part. Are we therefore producing generations of socially distressed misfits who pay the price for their parents' selfishness? It all depends on where you stand—both personally and politically. Those with direct experience of divorce understand that this is an immensely fraught and complex issue with no easy answers. Those with a political axe to grind cite various surveys to show that divorce inevitably damages children. In a right-wing scenario, divorce is the product of a quest for individual gratification at the expense of the well-being of children. It is part of modern society's inability to compromise personal happiness for the sake of the social good. I have always rather liked social commentator Auberon Waugh's comment that the children of divorced parents should be put to death, as it seems the logical conclusion of much Conservative huffing and puffing. Those who want to find fuel for this argument need only read author Hanif Kureishi's recent novella, *Intimacy*. Here they can find almost a parody of a self-obsessed and immature man who leaves his partner and children because he really is an existentialist, and really has a younger girlfriend.

The "liberal" view on divorce, which obviously I share, though divorce is not a personal favourite of mine, is one I would categorise as pro-choice. Divorce is a fact of life and clearly related to female economic independence. People get out of marriages in greater numbers than ever before because they can afford to. I do not see how couples who loathe each other can be persuaded to stay together for the sake of the children although, of course, I know of arrangements in which this supposedly works. One of my best friends was brought up by parents who never spoke to each other directly. I would not describe her as the best adjusted of people. In fact some of the maddest characters I have ever encountered were once the very children that their parents stayed together "for the sake of".

Over the years, though, everyone has latched on to certain pieces of research to shore up their own feelings about divorce. A new study produced by the Joseph Rowntree Foundation serves a useful purpose in reviewing 200 studies from the last three decades. Some of them contradict each other, some have no control groups or are based on tiny samples, some are inconclusive. Overwhelmingly, however, I would suggest that they tell us what we already know. First, it's impossible to isolate the one factor in a child's life that serves as a sole cause of disadvantage. Do the children of divorce suffer more because they are likely to be living with their mothers on less money and in poorer housing, or because they are emotionally traumatised by their parents' separation? Where the report is useful, is in dispelling certain myths about divorce. It does not appear to be true, for instance, that boys are more severely affected and therefore more inclined to be delinquent than girls; it's just that in the general population boys are more inclined to be delinquent than girls. When children do appear to suffer it is more to do with material deprivation than with divorce. The Rowntree report finds, when it compares educational attainment of the children of "intact families" to the children of divorced families, that there is no real difference when socioeconomic factors have been taken into account. In the words of the report, there is "no simple or direct relationship between parental separation and children's adjustment".

The Problems Point to Poverty

The glaring subtext of this study is that what is bad for children is not divorce but poverty. I think it is important that we understand this. Instead of having government increasingly trying to regulate our private lives and various moralists trying to turn the clock back, we need to realise that the impoverishment of women and children has to be addressed if we really do care about the future of our children.

"Heads! She gets the house!"

We more or less know already what a "good" divorce is. Those who view divorce as a process rather than a single event are more likely to be able to support their children. Conflict, rather than separation itself, is bad for children. Parental death does not carry the same risks for children as divorce. Most children wish that their parents could stay together but if they can't, they want to maintain contact with both parents. The quality of that contact is as important as the quantity. Younger children tend to fare better than older ones, but those who fare best are those who are told what is going on. The development of non-adversarial techniques for parents is extremely important if divorcing couples are not to end up divorcing their children.

It is also easier for children today in that they are less stigmatised by their parent's separation. When I fell over at school my PE teacher was so shocked that I had a different surname to my mother's, as she had remarried, that instead of taking me to hospital she quizzed me about what it was like to come from a "broken home". Was it painful? Yes, I eventually screamed, for I was less concerned about my broken home than my broken wrist.

Step-Family Scars

What this study inadvertently highlights is not just the effect of divorce but the reality of Nineties Britain, where increasing numbers of children live in step-families. Adults may create step-families in the hope that they will simply replicate and replace nuclear families. This is not the case, and step-families may not always be good for children. Indeed, many studies find that children are likely to do better in lone-parent families than they are in step-families. Inevitably, as serial monogamy takes over, the step-family will be increasingly common. In the US, which has a lower divorce rate than Britain's, it is estimated that one third of all children will be stepchildren.

It is this, I suggest, that we should concentrate on when we look seriously at the consequences of divorce. The restructuring of families, as well as their breakdown, can be damaging. Though this may be the way we live now, there is still little acknowledgement of the real diversity of family life.

Pundits and politicians still talk of the undermining of family life and marriage as though family life meant exactly the same thing to everyone. Yet who are these people who split up and reconstitute themselves, if not families? We need to learn how to make up families as well as how to tear them apart, for divorce is no longer the final curtain, just the end of the first act.

> *"Working moms are at the very center of a variety of cultural ills."*

Working Mothers Are Harming the Family

Richard Lowry

According to Richard Lowry, most women would like to stay home and care for their children, but society pressures them into believing that a career is more important than family. He argues that society should support women who choose to raise their children full time instead of women who abandon their children to day care providers. Lowry is an editor at the *National Review*, a conservative national magazine.

As you read, consider the following questions:
1. Why does the author think career moms need to be "coddled"?
2. According to Lowry, where does career mothers' guilt come from?
3. What does Francis Fukuyama associate with women's liberation and family breakdown?

Richard Lowry, "Nasty, Brutish, and Short," *National Review*, Vol. 53, May 28, 2001, pp. 36–42. Copyright © 2001 by *National Review*. Reproduced with permission.

Contemporary culture values sensitivity and softness, the "nice" virtues, above almost all else: except, we have now learned, when it comes to one particular segment of the population. These are preschoolers who spend more than thirty hours a week in day care. They, it turns out, can possess all the fierceness of Scottish rebel William Wallace, and most of the nation's cultural pooh-bahs will pronounce themselves well pleased. The new appreciation of aggressiveness comes in response to the now-infamous national study finding that long stretches away from a mother's care tend to make toddlers more aggressive and defiant.

This study, by the National Institute of Child Health and Human Development (NICHD), reports that kids in nonmaternal care tend to be associated with qualities such as "gets in lots of fights," "cruelty," "explosive behavior," "talking too much," "argues a lot," and "demands a lot of attention." *Time* magazine, reflecting the line taken by many liberal commentators, responded this way: "Should we even be worried at all? The researchers noted that almost all the 'aggressive' toddlers were well within the range of normal behavior for four-year-olds. And what about that adjective, anyway? Is a vice not sometimes a form of virtue? Cruelty never is, but arguing back? Is that being defiant—or spunky and independent? Demanding attentions could be a natural and healthy skill to develop if you are in a room with 16 other kids." And getting in fights? Explosive behavior?

This line is in keeping with a tendency in academia and the media to find a way to pronounce anything associated with day care—up to and including infectious illness—a good thing, so as to shield working mothers from any bad news. Career moms need such coddling for a reason. Mothers who choose to work full-time jobs and routinely leave their young children with others for much of the day are not normal: They are a historical aberration; they represent a minority preference among women; and they run exactly counter to the standard of motherhood that should be encouraged by society. No wonder elite culture treats them as hothouse flowers, who must hear nary a discouraging word. But the fact is that working moms are at the very center of a variety of cultural ills. Maybe a little stigma is exactly what they deserve. . . .

Where Does Guilt Come From?

Work has, in post-feminist America, become central to the identity of women (and child-rearing doesn't count). Work is an act of historical redemption for all those centuries of oppression and sexism, so that sounding at all skeptical about it is to be identified with those former forces of darkness. When negative day care studies appear, there's a palpable worry, not that the children are endangered, but that women's careers are. Time.com ran a piece dismissing the NICHD study "in an effort to keep half of America's workforce from running screaming from their offices." Author Susan Chira captured the work-as-redemption sentiment perfectly in her *A Mother's Place: Choosing Work and Family Without Guilt or Blame*, as she described the release that came with leaving her newborn at home: "When I returned to work [full time], I left behind a gnawing sense of oppression, boredom, and guilt that had cast a pall over my maternity leave" (her maternity leave had been six months long; she took an 18-month leave to write her book).

As the subtitle of Chira's book suggests, avoiding guilt and bad feelings is an obsession for working moms. But where does this guilt come from? Is there one television show, for example, that portrays working mothers in anything but a heroic light? No, this guilt must be something working mothers conjure themselves, some tickle in the back of their brains saying that they shouldn't be abandoning their children for much of the day. (For a snapshot of the sheer physical alienation that leaving a young child at home entails, consider this passage from Brian Robertson's *There's No Place Like Work*: "Almost three hundred American employers, including Aetna, Eastman Kodak, Cigna, and Home Depot, now offer 'lactation support rooms' where female employees can take regular breaks to attach electric pumps to their breasts in order to collect the milk in bottles for their infants in day care. Some companies, aside from the 'pumping rooms,' have 'lactation consultants' to help mothers solve breast-feeding problems.")

The media are wary of reporting negative day care results partly out of a fear of offending working mothers, but partly also out of tribal loyalty: Many of the reporters are themselves working moms (including Chira, who reported on day care for the *New York Times* while experiencing its joys). This produces reliably biased reporting. David Murray of the Statistical Assessment Service has written about a characteristic episode. A study in the *New England Journal of Medicine* found that kids who attended day care in their first six months were less likely to have asthma at age 13. The theory was that by being exposed to so many germs and infections so early, the kids developed resistance. The *Boston Globe*, the *New York Times*, and the *Washington Post* trumpeted the study. The *New England Journal* editorialized: "For those of us who share the furtive guilt of having left marginally ill toddlers at day care, these findings . . . offer a sense of relief." . . .

A Downward Spiral

Day care is the focus of much of the debate over working mothers, but the issue runs much deeper. The mass entry of women into the workforce has acted to dissolve the family in general. Once a woman is earning a salary comparable to a man's, marriage becomes economically less important while the opportunity cost of having children goes up (bearing a child will mean lost wages). Bottom line: As Francis Fukuyama points out in *The Great Disruption*, "substantial empirical evidence links higher female earnings to both divorce and extramarital childbearing." Just the specter of divorce creates a kind of intra-marital arms race. The wife works to hedge against getting abandoned, but her very act of working, research shows, makes it more likely that the marriage will fail—a dismaying downward spiral.

The old economic regime in which men worked and many women didn't was partly an informal bargain, but also the product of frank sex discrimination. One doesn't have to denigrate the new freedoms won for women when this regime collapsed to acknowledge that there was a dear cost to its passing. Francis Fukuyama connects women's liberation and the attendant family breakdown with the broader social disruption—higher rates of crime, illegitimacy, and distrust of institutions—that has affected the developed world over the last thirty years. The exception was Japan. What made it different? In part, it was a longstanding law passed in the 1940s that forbade women from working more than six hours of overtime a week, effectively barring women from participation in the most productive, overtime-dependent portion of the Japanese economy. It wasn't until 1986 that the law was lifted for white-collar workers, and not until 1997 (!) for blue-collar workers.

At Home and Loving It

All the books and studies in the world aren't strong enough to affect the reality and the joy of mothering. The mothers I know who "just" stay home are using all their education, patience, humor, love and insight to mother their children. . . . Sure, they'd like more respect, sure they'd probably like to afford more help with kids and housework or get more help from their husbands, but at the end of the day they feel good that they don't have to ask someone else how their child's day went. They understand what's going on in their children's lives and know that all too soon the little ones will go to school and be away from them most of the time (unless they are so fed up with the experts that they homeschool!). They know they can never get the early years back.

There is really no "just" in staying at home: it's a challenge, and it's more worthwhile than a thousand other jobs I could think of. To end with author George Gilder: "Only a specific woman can bear a specific child, and her tie to it is personal and infrangible. When she raises the child she imparts in privacy her own individual values. She can create children who transcend consensus and prefigure the future: children of private singularity rather than 'child development policy.'" Amen.

Maria McFadden, *Human Life Review*, Spring 1998.

Returning to a regime that discourages women's work as a matter of law is, of course, out of the question. But at the very least young women shouldn't be constantly told that they should want what they don't. Indeed, vestigial motherly urges have proved an insuperable obstacle to the full achievement of the feminist project. Ann Crittenden in her new book *The Price of Motherhood* details how women have voted with their feet to abandon the most ambitious goals of the feminists, after discovering that the most prestigious, high-pressure careers are simply incompatible with motherhood.

Crittenden reports that the representation of women in the top positions in law, accounting, science—you name it—has barely budged, because women tend to duck out of the labor force to have kids. Even in labor unions, which march in lockstep with the feminists, "less than 10 percent of top local officers are women, who are less likely to be married than their male counterparts." According to Crittenden, "The women without children have been twice as successful in achieving a career as the women with children." Nor have men begun to embrace the brave new role of housecleaners and nursemaids that feminists have outlined for them. Even when the wife earns more than half the family income, even when the husband is unemployed, he will typically pick up no more than 30 percent of housework and child-care duties.

What the feminist project is bumping up against, fundamentally, is the differing desires of the sexes. The survey data have told the story again and again: Most women value their children more than their careers, and would prefer to create a life for themselves that reflects this preference. As Brian Robertson points out, "Americans now assert, by a margin of two to one, that they would prefer to be a part of a one-earner couple rather than a two-earner couple." According to a nonpartisan Public Agenda survey in 2000, roughly 80 percent of parents with children five and younger say a stay-at-home parent is best able to give children the "affection and attention they need." Roughly 70 percent of today's young mothers call day care centers the "option of last resort." The day care revolution, it seems, is hardly riding a wave of popular support.

How Inevitable?

Feminists counter such data with the argument that working mothers are economically inevitable. As Ann Hulbert has written in the *New Republic*, "the two-paycheck family, as even its detractors increasingly admit, is largely the product of economic necessity." Yes, wages for men stagnated for a period beginning in the mid 1970s. Yes, single mothers have to work. But day care isn't primarily for single moms. According to the Heritage Foundation's Robert Rector, "Nearly 80 percent of the preschool children using any form of day care come from married-couple families with two income earners." And women married to men up and down the income scale avail themselves of day care—it's not necessarily an economics-driven choice. It is odd indeed that so many mothers are supposedly forced into the workforce when American society is so much richer than in the 1950s, an "affluent society" that would seem hopelessly penurious today. . . .

Any measure to make it easier for women to stay at home would imply that there is something valuable in a mother's caring for her own child. It might, in other words, reflect poorly on those professional moms who really do have a choice whether to work or not—and this is one of our culture's most sacred taboos. As feminist Katha Pollitt recently wrote, "The truth is, the day care debate has always been about college-educated working moms." So it has. And it is to their whims, to their career ambitions and their uneasy consciences, that federal policy and the culture have been bent. Indeed, in this light, the saccharine worry about "the children" in American culture and politics seems a guilty overcompensation. We are willing to do anything "for the children" except suggest that their mothers should stay with them; we are committed to "leaving no child behind" unless it is by his mother hustling off to make her career.

Yes, a mother staying at home must make painful sacrifices, sacrifices that most men will never know. But isn't that more reason to celebrate this choice rather than shun it, to make it easier rather than harder? When it comes to the American family, the policy, the stigma—everything tilts the wrong way. Why shouldn't working moms feel guilty, especially if they share a shred of the sentiment expressed by their boosters like Susan Chira? "It is a parent's responsibility to curb children's natural fantasy that they are the center of the universe," she writes in her book. "A mother who never says, 'No, I can't, because this is my time now,' is a mother who convinces children she lives only for them." Funny. Not too long ago that was what a mother's love was supposed to be all about.

| *"Working mothers have become the norm."*

Working Mothers Are Benefiting the Family

Reed Karaim

In the following viewpoint, Reed Karaim argues that working mothers teach their children to be independent, curious, and ambitious. He maintains that children of working mothers do not suffer from less parental attention than children whose mothers stay home. Rather, children whose mothers work learn the value of personal fulfillment and goal-setting. Karaim is the author of the novel *If Men Were Angels.*

As you read, consider the following questions:

1. According to the author, why was the transformation to parenthood more difficult for his female friends than his male friends?
2. How do working mothers counter popular culture, as stated by the author?
3. According to Karaim, how do most children of working mothers feel about their mothers' choice?

Like many ambitious baby boomers in Washington, most of my friends married in their thirties and didn't get around to having children until that decade was ending or over. They went from being successful two-career couples, happily scaling the ladder of professional achievement together, chatting about work over dinner in Georgetown at 10 P.M., to that sudden, startling state known as parenthood.

More Difficult for Women

The transformation was shocking all around (diapers, not dinner, at 10; Gymboree, not the gym, on weekends) but the most difficult adjustment inevitably was for my female friends. Successful editors, publicists, political consultants, women whose confidence and accomplishment had seemed unwavering, were suddenly uncertain about their futures.

How devoted could they or should they remain to work? Were they hurting their children—socially, academically— by pursuing a career? In some cases, soaring professional trajectories were abandoned, part-time arrangements found, accommodations made—out of desire, yes, but also out of fear or guilt.

I understood better when my wife and I had our own daughter, a little later than most of our friends, and began pondering day care. "Of course, it's best if they can stay home with their mother," we heard too many times, as if parental roles had been perfected in the 1950s.

It wasn't as if people were rude enough to suggest this was what we should do. Most were too sensitive, or aware that we needed my wife's income. Rather, it was as if there were an implicit understanding that a mother and child, at home, together, was the ideal situation and all else was, at best, an accommodation, a compromise.

As the grown son of a mother who worked his whole childhood, I've always been offended by this attitude. Now, as the husband of a working mom, I feel more than ever that it's misguided and damaging. Watching my own wife struggle with her sense that she might be cheating our daughter, watching friends exhaust themselves trying to do it all, I think it's time we both recognize that working mothers have become the norm and celebrate all that they can actually bring to their children's lives.

According to Department of Labor statistics from 1999, 72 percent of all women with children under age 18 work. Even most moms with infants work: 61 percent of all mothers with children under the age of 3. This isn't going to change. We are several years into an economic boom of historic proportions; if ever there was a time working mothers were going to retire from the job force, this would be it. Yet the percentage of working mothers continued to climb throughout the '90s. The Beaver's mom has left a casserole in the refrigerator and gone off to work. She'll try to be home by 6.

What is her family getting in return? For starters, quite often the answer is the groceries and a roof over their heads. The money working mothers make is tremendously important to their families. Two-parent families where the mother works have an average annual income of $63,751, $26,000 more a year than households where only the father works. In most of America, this extra income may not seem extravagant, but it helps boost many families onto the verdant green lawns of the middle class, with all the comforts, chances for education and opportunity that provides to children.

Somehow this gets neglected in the various academic studies that seek to determine whether the children of working mothers do worse than their peers, either socially or academically. The studies disagree. But there's one thing we can be sure of—the money matters.

Setting a Good Example

Something else that matters is the example we set our children. And one important example is a willingness to work. There's no one who doesn't need to learn this sooner or later, and it's a lesson taught best by example.

If a mother is lucky enough to have a job she enjoys (and, while many of us like to complain about our work, the truth is that most people do like their jobs, at least a little), she provides her children a valuable window into some of the fulfillment possible in adult life.

A working mother can teach the value of independence, first through her own life, and second by expecting her children to take on more themselves. There is struggle in that, yes, but handled right, there can be pride and accomplishment.

I know this will upset some parents, but I think the children of working mothers can occasionally even enjoy a valuable sense of freedom. As a teenager, I remember visiting friends whose mothers seemed way too wrapped up in their high school lives. I found myself glad my own mother was too busy to worry about whether I had a chance of being elected prom king. (I didn't.)

Problems with Staying Home

This generation has been raised to be financially self-reliant and part of the working world. That's why women put themselves emotionally at risk when they trade in their work identity for full-time motherhood. A mother who stays home for five to ten years to raise her children may gradually feel off-balance or depressed by the loss of her former "working" self. Later, she may regret that unfulfilled potential and project her need to achieve onto her child.

Many woman do decide to stay home to raise children, but often that's because our overdrive culture asks them to choose between "cold careerist" or "devoted mother." They simply can't think of how to have both work and family, especially if their husbands haven't adjusted their work so they can parent too.

Many other women, even successful ones, are unconsciously so ambivalent about competing in the "masculine" world of work, they use motherhood as an excuse to drop out. But whatever the reason, if a woman does stay home, she should be aware ahead of time that her marriage will not remain equal if she has no income, nor will her future be secure should she divorce. So full-time mothers should plan to remain financially self-reliant and maintain some access to work rather than just drop out totally. If they carve out space for their own pursuits, they will also be less resentful and enjoy motherhood more.

Joan K. Peters, *When Mothers Work: Loving Our Children Without Sacrificing Ourselves*, 1998.

A working mother, unless she happens to make her living as a swimsuit model, stands as a counterweight to a popular culture that still teaches us to value women more for how they fill out a sweater than a resume. This is obviously important to daughters, but often overlooked is how important it is to sons.

I look at my own mother, who raised seven children while working as a college teacher and librarian, and I think this is one of the great favors she did me. I saw her in charge. I saw her debating things with my father, also a teacher, as an equal, personally, professionally and financially. I marched off into adult life thinking this was the way things were, and I and the succession of female bosses I've had all had our lives made easier.

Encouraging Their Children's Dreams

Finally, successful working mothers give their children one of the best gifts any parent can, the example of a life lived to its potential. Ambition and achievement are contagious, and we all need role models to encourage our dreams.

This is not to say it's easy, or to dismiss the understandable difficulty of leaving a child and going back to work, or to suggest that our society couldn't do more to support working parents. Nor is it to say that mothers who stay home with their children are limiting themselves; there can be rewards and growth there aplenty. Nothing here is intended to disparage women, or men for that matter, who make that choice.

It is only to say that a working mother need not feel guilty. The pseudo-Victorians and Eisenhower-era nostalgics who wonder how this generation of children will grow up without mom at home with them all day are so in love with a sepia-toned still life that they've missed the bigger picture. As a parent, it's the whole life you bring to your child that matters.

Children understand this better than we think. A 1997 national survey by Massachusetts Mutual Life Insurance of 800 15- to 31-year-olds whose mothers worked found that 80 percent thought their mothers made the right choice. An even higher percentage, 82 percent, thought their moms enjoyed their jobs.

I knew my own mother did, and as a child it made me happy. The world seemed full of greater possibility because of it: Her interest in books was contagious; the way she enjoyed her days at the library made me eager to get out into the larger world of ideas and people. Did I feel adequately loved? Valued? Of course. But I also knew there were things that mattered beside me, and that they involved work, but they were worth it.

Someday my daughter will be paying attention when her mother comes home after a good day of teaching creative writing, something my wife loves, and will feel that same contagious joy and sense of possibility. She will be a lucky child. Because her mother works.

Periodical Bibliography

The following articles have been selected to supplement the diverse views presented in this chapter.

Anne Applebaum "Tell the Truth About Babies," *New Statesman*, August 28, 1998.

Lynette Burrows "Suffer, the Children," *Human Life Review*, Spring 1999.

Ilene Chaykin "Babes in Arm," *Los Angeles Magazine*, July 2000.

Frank F. Furstenberg "Is the Modern Family a Threat to Children's Health?" *Society*, July/August 1999.

Terry Golway "The End of the Family?" *America*, July 16, 2001.

E.J. Graff "The Other Marriage War," *American Prospect*, April 8, 2002.

Megan Rutherford "When Mother Stays Home: Who Are the Women Who Leave Their Jobs to Raise Kids, and What Are Their Most Pressing Concerns?" *Time*, October 16, 2000.

Louise B. Silverstein and Carl F. Auerbach "The Myth of the 'Normal' Family," *USA Today Magazine*, January 2001.

Maria Stainer "Children and Families," *World & I*, October 1999.

Ed Vitagliano "What Is a Family?" *American Family Association Journal*, March 2001.

Helen Wilkinson "Celebrate the New Family," *New Statesman*, August 9, 1999.

Robert L. Woodson "Breaking the Cycle of Family Dissolution— Against the Greatest Odds," *World & I*, June 2001.

CHAPTER 2

Is Marriage Necessary for Healthy Families?

Chapter Preface

Commenting on the changes that the institution of marriage has undergone over the last century, legal scholar John Witte observed, "The early Enlightenment ideals of marriage as a permanent contractual union designed for the sake of mutual love, procreation and protection is slowly giving way to a new reality of marriage as a 'terminal sexual contract' designed for the gratification of the individual parties."

Certain grim statistics seem to support Witte's statement: About two and a half million Americans divorce each year, and nearly 50 percent of marriages in the United States end in divorce or separation within fifteen years. Moreover, the incidence of divorce increased more than sixfold since the early twentieth century. Many marriage supporters argue that the women's rights movement in the 1960s and 1970s contributed to the decline of the marriage institution by changing women's focus from their families to themselves.

In 1963, Betty Friedan, in her controversial book *The Feminine Mystique*, documented the emotional and intellectual frustration many women were experiencing because society expected them to become mothers and housewives. Many women in America identified with the sentiments expressed in *The Feminine Mystique*, and the publication of the book was one of many events that facilitated women's quest for educational, social, and workplace equality. In 1964, Congress passed the Civil Rights Act, which prohibited discrimination on the basis of sex, race, religion, or national origin. In 1972, Title IX in the Education Codes gave women equal access to higher education. These legislative acts freed women to explore avenues of personal fulfillment that were unknown to their mothers or grandmothers.

Whereas in the past, women were expected to embrace predetermined roles as homemakers and mothers, the women's rights movement allowed women to choose what they wished to become. Perhaps more significantly, by working, women gained hitherto unknown monetary independence and were no longer financially dependent upon their husbands. Many women chose to leave abusive or unsatisfying marriages, and the divorce rate skyrocketed. These divorces created an abundance of single-parent homes, second marriages, and step-parented families. Critics of the women's movement contend that many mothers began to focus on their personal satisfaction at the expense of their children's right to a stable, traditional family.

However, these critics fail to acknowledge that the women's movement benefited children enormously by providing them with mothers who could teach their children independence, determination, and ambition. Daughters can now learn to be assertive and competitive, and sons can learn to respect women as whole human beings equal to men. Moreover, children who see their parents demand personal satisfaction in their careers and marriages are more likely to seek fulfillment in their own lives than children whose parents were disappointed in life and lived unhappily. Indeed, contrary to what John Witte believed, men and women today are more likely to require personal contentment and will therefore enter into marriages that reflect the Enlightenment ideal of "mutual love, procreation and protection."

"Married men and women do better than those who are unmarried."

Marriage Leads to Healthier Families

Linda J. Waite

The number of people who marry in their lifetime has declined since 1950, and an increasing number of couples are cohabiting—living together in a sexual relationship without being married—before marriage or in lieu of marriage. In the following article, Linda J. Waite contends that the decline of marriage is a problem because marriage offers considerable benefits to couples and their children. She argues that married people enjoy better health, longer lives, more satisfactory sex, higher wages, and greater wealth than unmarried people. Moreover, children of married people do better in school and are less likely to be poor than children of unmarried people. Waite concludes that society should endorse public policies that support marriage. Waite is a sociology professor and the co-author of *The Case for Marriage: Why Married People Are Healthier, Happier, and Better Off Financially*.

As you read, consider the following questions:
1. According to the author, how does marriage affect problem drinking?
2. In what three ways does marriage lengthen life, as stated by Waite?
3. Why does being married increase men's wages, according to the author?

Linda J. Waite, "The Importance of Marriage Is Being Overlooked," *USA Today*, January 1999, pp. 46–47. Copyright © 1999 by Society for the Advancement of Education. Reproduced with permission.

M arriage seems to be less popular with Americans now than in the past. Men and women are marrying for the first time at much older ages than their parents did. They are divorcing more and living together more often and for longer periods. Perhaps most troubling, they are becoming unmarried parents at record rates.

What are the implications, for individuals, of these increases in nonmarriage? If marriage is thought of as an insurance policy—which the institution is, in some respects—does it matter if more people are uninsured or are insured with a term rather than a whole-life policy?

It does matter, because marriage typically provides important and substantial benefits, to individuals as well as society. Marriage improves the health and longevity of men and women; gives them access to a more active and satisfying sex life; increases wealth and assets; boosts children's chances for success; and enhances men's performance at work and their earnings.

A quick look at marriage patterns today compared to, say, 1950 illustrates the extent of recent changes. Figures from the Census Bureau show that, at the height of the baby boom, about one-third of adult whites were not married. Some were waiting to marry for the first time; others were divorced or widowed and not remarried. Nevertheless, most Americans married at least once at some point in their lives, generally in their early 20s.

In 1950, the proportion of black adults not married was approximately equal to that among whites, but since that time, marriage behavior of blacks and whites has diverged dramatically. By 1993, 61% of black women and 58% of black men were not married, compared to 38% of white men and 41% of white women. In contrast to 1950, when slightly over one black adult in three was not married, a majority of black adults are unmarried today. Insofar as marriage "matters," black men and women are much less likely than whites to share in the benefits than they were even a generation ago.

The Rise in Cohabitation

The decline in marriage intimately is connected to the rise in cohabitation—living with someone in a sexual relationship without being married. Although Americans are less likely to be wed today than they were several decades ago, if both marriage and cohabitation are counted, they are about as likely to be "coupled." If cohabitation provides the same benefits to individuals marriage does, then is it necessary to be concerned about this shift? Yes, because a valuable social institution arguably is being replaced by one that demands and offers less.

Perhaps the most disturbing change in marriage appears in its relationship to parenthood. Today, a third of all births occur to women who are not married, with huge, but shrinking, differences between blacks and whites in this behavior. One-fifth of births to white mothers and two-thirds of births to blacks currently take place outside marriage. Although about a quarter of the white unmarried mothers are living with someone when they give birth, so that their children are born into two-parent—if unmarried—families, very few black children born to unwed mothers live with their fathers, too.

These changes in marriage behavior are a cause for concern because, on a number of important dimensions, married men and women do better than those who are unmarried. The evidence suggests that is because they are married.

Healthy Behaviors

Married people tend to lead healthier lives than otherwise similar men and women who are not. For example, a 1997 national survey about problem drinking during the past year compared the prevalence of this unhealthy behavior among divorced, widowed, and married men and women. Problem drinking was defined as drinking more than subjects planned to, failing to do things they should have done because of drinking, and/or drinking to the point of hurting their health. Responses showed much lower rates of problem drinking for married than for unmarried men and extremely low reports of this condition for married or unmarried women. Excessive drinking seems to be a particularly male pattern of social pathology, one that females generally manage to avoid.

However, unmarried women report higher levels of other unhealthy acts than married women, in particular "risk-taking behavior." Risk-taking reflects accidents around the house, while in the car, or on the job caused by carelessness; taking chances by driving too fast or doing things that might endanger others; and/or having serious arguments or fights at home or outside the home. Males and females reveal similar levels of risk-taking on national surveys, but married men and women reflect much lower levels than those who are divorced. . . .

How does marriage affect healthy behaviors? It provides individuals—especially men—with someone who monitors their health and health-related behaviors and encourages them to drink and smoke less, eat a healthier diet, get enough sleep, and generally take care of their health. In addition, husbands and wives offer each other moral support that helps in dealing with stressful situations. Married men especially seem to be motivated to avoid risky behaviors and take care of their health by the sense of meaning that marriage gives to their lives and the sense of obligation to others that it brings.

Mortality

Married men and women appear to live healthier lives. Perhaps as a result, they face lower risks of dying at any point than those who never have married or whose previous marriage has ended.

With RAND Corporation economist Lee Lillard, I used a large national survey—the Panel Study of Income Dynamics—to follow men and women over a 20-year period. We watched them get married, get divorced, and remarry. We observed the death of spouses and of the individuals themselves. When we compared deaths of married men and women to those who were not married, we found that, once other factors were taken into account, the former show the lowest chances of dying. Widowed women were much better off than divorced women or those who never have married, although they still were disadvantaged when compared with married women. All men who were not married currently faced higher risks of dying than married men, regardless of their marital history. Other researchers have found similar differentials in death rates for unmarried adults in a number of countries besides the U.S.

How does marriage reduce the risk of dying and lengthen

life? First, it appears to reduce risky and unhealthy behaviors. Second, it increases material well-being—income, assets, and wealth. These can be used to purchase better medical care, a healthier diet, and safer surroundings, all of which lengthen life. This material improvement seems to be especially important for women. Third, marriage provides individuals with a network of help and support, with others who rely on them and on whom they can rely. This seems to be especially important for men. Marriage also provides adults with an on-site, readily available sex partner.

Sexual Satisfaction

In 1991, a national survey research organization conducted the National Health and Social Life Survey on a probability sample of 3,432 adults. It asked, among other things, how often they had sex with a partner. Married respondents reported levels of sexual activity about twice as high as singles. Married men cited a mean frequency of sexual activity of 6.8 times and single men 3.6 times per month over the last year. Married women indicated a mean of 6.1 times and single women 3.2 times per month over the last year. Cohabiting men and women also reported higher rates of sexual activity—7.4 and 7.2 times per month, respectively, over the past year—suggesting that, as far as sexual activity, cohabitation surpasses marriage in its benefits to the individuals involved.

I also examined levels of physical satisfaction people cited from sex with their husband or wife, their cohabiting partner, or the primary partner identified by singles and found that married men more often said that sex with their wives was extremely pleasurable than cohabiting men or single men indicated that sex with their partners was. The high level of married men's physical satisfaction with their sex lives contradicts the popular view that sexual newness or variety improves sex for men. Physical satisfaction with sex is about the same for married women, cohabiting women, and single women with sex partners.

In addition to reporting more active sex lives than singles, married men and women say they are more emotionally satisfied with their sex lives than do those who are single or cohabiting. Although cohabitors report levels of sexual activity slightly higher than married people, both cohabiting men and women cite lower levels of satisfaction with their sex lives. In all comparisons where there is a difference, the married are more satisfied than the unmarried.

How does marriage improve one's sex life? Marriage and cohabitation provide individuals with a readily available sexual partner with whom they have an established, ongoing sexual relationship. Since married couples expect to carry on their sex lives for many years, and since most married couples are monogamous, husbands and wives have strong incentives to learn what pleases their partner in bed and to become good at it. Then, sex with a partner who knows what one likes and how to provide it becomes more satisfying than sex with a partner who lacks such skills. The emotional ties that exist in marriage increase sexual activity and satisfaction with it as well.

Assets and Wealth

In addition to having more sex, married couples have more money. Household wealth—one comprehensive measure of financial well-being—includes pension plans and Social Security, real and financial assets, and the value of the primary residence. According to RAND economist James Smith, married men and women age 51–60 had median wealth in 1992 of about $66,000, compared to $42,000 for the widowed, $35,000 for those who never had married, $34,000 among those who were divorced, and $7,600 for those who were separated. Although married couples have higher incomes than others, this fact accounts for just about a quarter of their greater wealth.

Married couples can share many household goods and services, such as a television set and heat, so the cost to each individual is lower than if each one purchased and used the same items individually. Thus, they spend less than they would for the same style of life if they lived separately. Second, married people produce more than the same individuals would if they were single. Each spouse can develop some skills and neglect others, because he or she can count on the other to take responsibility for some of the household work. The resulting specialization increases efficiency and, as will be shown, leads to higher wages for men. Moreover, married couples seem to save more at the same level of income than singles.

Children's Well-Being

To this point, we have focused on the consequences of marriage for adults—the men and women who choose to marry (and stay married) or not—but these choices have consequences for the children borne by these adults as well. Sociologists Sara McLanahan and Gary Sandefur compared children raised in intact, two-parent families with those raised in one-parent families, resulting either from disruption of a marriage or from unmarried childbearing. They found that approximately twice as many teenagers raised in one-parent families drop out of high school without finishing. Children raised in one-parent families are more likely to become mothers or fathers while teenagers and to be "idle"—both out of school and out of the labor force—as young adults.

Youngsters living outside an intact marriage are more likely to be poor. McLanahan and Sandefur calculated poverty rates for children in two-parent families—including stepfamilies—and for single-parent families. They found very high rates of poverty for single-parent families, especially among blacks. Donald Hernandez, chief of marriage and family statistics at the Census Bureau, estimates that the rise in mother-only families since 1959 is an important cause of increases in poverty among children. Clearly, poverty, in and of itself, is a bad outcome for kids. . . .

Single-parent families and stepfamilies move much more frequently than two-parent families. These moves are extremely difficult for kids, both academically and socially. Finally, individuals who spent part of their childhood in a single-parent family, either because they were born to an unmarried mother or because their parents divorced, report substantially lower-quality relationships with their parents as adults and have less frequent contact with them, according to University of Washington demographer Diane Lye.

Labor Force and Career

Wharton School economist Kermit Daniel has examined the difference in the wages of young men and women who are single, cohabiting, and married, once one takes into account other characteristics that might affect salaries, and labels the remaining difference a "wage premium" for marriage. He finds that both black and white men receive a wage premium if they are married: 4.5% for blacks and 6.3% for whites. Black women receive a marriage premium of almost three percent. White women, however, pay a marriage penalty, in hourly wages, of more than four percent. Men appear to receive some of the benefit of marriage if they cohabitate, but women do not.

For women, Daniel finds that marriage and presence of children together seem to affect wages, and the effects depend on the woman's race. Childless black women earn substantially more money if they are married, but the marriage premium drops with each kid they have. Among white women, just the childless receive a marriage premium. Once white women become mothers, marriage decreases their earnings compared to remaining single (without children), with very large negative effects of marriage on females' earnings for those with two offspring or more. White married women often choose to reduce hours of work when they have children. They make less per hour than either unmarried mothers or childless wives.

Why should being married increase men's wages? Some researchers think that it makes men more productive at work, leading to higher wages. Wives may assist husbands directly with their work, offer advice or support, or take over household tasks, freeing their spouses' time and energy for work. As mentioned earlier, being married reduces drinking, substance abuse, and other unhealthy behaviors that may affect men's job performance. Finally, marriage increases men's incentives to perform well at work, so as to meet obligations to family members. . . .

Is Marriage Responsible?

The obvious question, when one looks at all these benefits of marriage, is whether marriage is responsible for the differences. If all, or almost all, arise because those who enjoy better health, live longer lives, or earn higher wages anyway are more likely to marry, then marriage is not "causing" any changes in these outcomes. Social scientists vigorously and often acrimoniously debate the extent to which marriage is responsible for these better outcomes.

When politicians point to the high social costs and taxpayer burdens imposed by disintegrating "family values," they overlook the fact that individuals do not make the decisions that lead to unwed parenthood, marriage, or divorce on the basis of what is good for society. They weigh the costs and benefits of each of these choices to themselves—and sometimes their children.

Social scientists have a responsibility to measure the evidence on the consequences of social behaviors in the same way as medical researchers evaluate the evidence on the consequences of, say, cigarette smoking or exercise. As evidence accumulates and is communicated to the public, some people will change their behavior as a result. Some will make different choices than they otherwise would have because of their understanding of the costs and benefits, to them, of the options involved.

To continue with the example of medical issues such as smoking or exercise, behaviors have been seen to change substantially because research findings have been communicated to the public. In addition, there have been changes in attitudes toward behaviors shown to have negative consequences, especially when those consequences affect others, as in the case of smoking. These attitude changes then raise the social cost of newly stigmatized behaviors. HMOs and religious organizations develop programs to help people achieve the desired behavior, and support groups spring up. . . .

If, as I have argued, marriage as a social institution produces individuals who drink, smoke, and abuse substances less, live longer, earn more, are wealthier, and have children who do better, society needs to give more thought and effort to supporting marriage through public policies.

"Marriage doesn't play the role it used to in most people's lives."

Marriage Is Not Necessary for Healthy Families

Dorian Solot

In the following viewpoint, Dorian Solot argues that unmarried couples can be as happy and healthy as married couples. According to Solot, some couples are unmarried because they choose to be, and other couples, such as homosexual couples, cannot marry. Solot contends that families would benefit if society banned discrimination—such as denying partners health benefits or preventing them from renting an apartment—against unmarried couples. Solot is the executive director of the Alternatives to Marriage Project and co-author of *Unmarried to Each Other: The Essential Guide to Living Together as an Unmarried Couple.*

As you read, consider the following questions:

1. According to the author, by what percentage has the number of unmarried partners grown between 1990 and 2000?
2. What are three reasons why people choose not to marry, as described by the author?
3. According to Solot, how can individuals make society more accepting of unmarried families?

Dorian Solot, "No Ring to It: Considering a Less-Married Future." A version of this article was originally written for "The Future of Family and Tribe," seminar at the Jewish Public Forum of the National Jewish Center for Learning and Leadership, January 28–29, 2002. Copyright © 2002 by Dorian Solot. Reproduced with permission.

W e'll start with a marriage quiz. Which of the following statements is true?

   a) 90% of Americans marry at some point in their lives.
   b) Most Americans spend the majority of their lives un-
      married.
   c) The marriage rate in the U.S. is significantly higher
      than marriage rates across Europe.
   d) The majority of Americans who marry today have
      lived together first.
   e) All of the above.

The answer is (e), all of the above—a collection of contradic-
tions. Americans love marriage to death, though not necessarily 'til death do we part. We love marriage so much that 9 out
of 10 of us marry in our lifetimes, and that movies that include
wedding scenes sell more tickets at the box office. We place so
much importance on the marriage ceremony itself that we delight in throwing the most lavish, elaborate weddings of any
culture in history, spending on the average wedding nearly the
amount the average American earns in a year. We have such
confidence in marriage that it is an unquestioned truism that
children do best in married parent families, and that President
George W. Bush has proposed promoting marriage among
people on welfare as a plausible solution to poverty.

Marriage's New Role

But even as the television show *Who Wants to Marry a Mil-
lionaire?* recently took the country by storm, 150 years of demographic trends paint a clear picture: marriage doesn't play
the role it used to in most people's lives. More than 3 in 7
American adults are not currently married, and at the rate of
increase of the last five decades, the bare ring finger crowd
will be a majority in a few decades. But even if we're not
marrying as soon or staying married as long, Americans are
forming relationships at about the same rate we always have;
the decrease in married couples is mostly offset by an increase in unmarried ones. In fact, unmarried partners are
one of the fastest-growing household types, increasing by
72% between 1990 and 2000. These unmarried partner
households don't necessarily fit the stereotype of a young,
childless couple either: 41% of them include children.

I'm part of this fast-growing constituency. I share my life and plans for the future with my partner of nine years. Our relationship is strong and committed; we take out the recycling and consider each other's parents our in-laws (or, jokingly, our "out-laws") just like the married couples on our block. But neither of us feels any desire to make a trip down the aisle.

A few years into our relationship, I was stunned at the pressure to marry directed at us from friends, family members, and even strangers. Growing up I was told, "You can be an astronaut! You can be President of the United States!" I was caught completely off guard to learn in my twenties that the one thing society considered set in stone was that I would become a wife. Even though our relationship worked so well, my partner and I ran into marital status discrimination everywhere we went. A landlord threatened not to rent to us. My employer told me Marshall and I couldn't get a joint health insurance policy, even though we'd been in a relationship longer than some of the married couples with joint policies. A tenants' insurance company told us we'd have to take out two policies and pay double what a married couple would.

Today, being unmarried is not just my personal identity, but also my professional one. As the Executive Director of the Alternatives to Marriage Project (AtMP), a national non-profit organization for unmarried people, I work full-time organizing the grassroots movement advocating for fairness and equality for people who choose not to marry, cannot marry, and live together before marriage. AtMP has over 4,000 households on its mailing list, representing every state in the country, and our staff, board, and members appear in the media hundreds of times each year to provide an unmarried perspective to news about marriage and non-marriage. When Reverend Jerry Falwell, the Family Research Council, or the Traditional Values Coalition are on national television commenting on the latest census figures or welfare proposals, we're often the ones sitting next to them providing analysis from a family diversity perspective.

Who Are the Unmarrieds?

The people the Alternatives to Marriage Project represents don't all look like Marshall and me. Although pundits often talk about marriage as an issue of morals and values, economics provides a more accurate framework for understanding. Poor people are much less likely to marry, for reasons ranging from an inability to afford keeping a chronically unemployed spouse around the house, to the realization that marrying a poor partner would likely put a permanent end to any dream of upward mobility. A vast body of research makes the links clear: when the country's economy improves, marriage rates go up. The same holds true on an individual level, where rising incomes make people more likely to marry. As the gap between rich and poor widens in the U.S., marriage patterns follow a similar pattern, leading demographer Frank Furstenberg to famously describe marriage as a "luxury consumer item" and cohabitation and single parenthood the "budget" approaches to family formation.

But the poor aren't the only ones not married. Many people are unmarried because they haven't met a partner they find worthy of a lifetime commitment, because they want to avoid the pain or expense of divorce, because they don't want the government to "regulate" their relationship, or because they don't plan to have children and see no other reason to wed. Same-sex couples can't marry anywhere in the country, and thousands of different-sex couples have chosen not to marry to avoid taking advantage of a privilege available only to some. Many senior citizens and disabled people would lose significant financial benefits (perhaps a pension from a previous spouse) if they married or remarried. Thanks to employment for women and the invention of TV dinners and washing machines for men, husbands and wives are no longer essential to survival.

For the most part, we unmarried folks do just fine, thank you. If we're in relationships our lives are more similar to married couples than different from them. But because of the ease with which couples move in together, many of us are surprised at the "marital status–ism" we encounter. The first problem is a lack of social support from families, communities, and religious institutions. It's widely believed that social support is a key ingredient to making marriages strong, yet cohabiting couples often see their partners excluded and relationships ignored at family events, and shamed or stigmatized in faith communities. Many describe the pressure to marry as intense (and without regard for whether marriage is in their best interest), and with it the message that their relationship as it currently stands is second best, inadequate. Legal barriers compound the problems. Everywhere that families come into contact with the law—housing, employment, health care, insurance, taxes, immigration, adoption, pensions, social security, inheritance, and more—the legal system is oblivious to the needs and realities of unmarried families.

Changing Times, Changing Families

There is no way to re-establish marriage as the main site of child rearing, dependent care, income pooling, or interpersonal commitments in the modern world. Any movement that sets this as a goal misunderstands how irreversibly family life and marriage have changed, and it will inevitably be dominated by powerful "allies" who are not interested in supporting the full range of families that exist today and are likely to in the future. For more than 1,000 years, marriage was the main way that society transferred property, forged political alliances, raised capital, organized children's rights, redistributed resources to dependents, and coordinated the division of labor by age and gender. Precisely because marriage served so many political, social, and economic functions, not everyone had access to it. Those who did almost never had free choice regarding partners and rarely could afford to hold high expectations of their relationships.

During the last 200 years, the growth of bureaucracies, banks, schools, hospitals, unemployment insurance, Social Security, and pension plans slowly but surely eroded the political and economic roles that marriage traditionally had played. It increasingly became an individual decision that could be made independently of family and community pressures. By the early 1900s, love and companionship had become not just the wistful hope of a husband or wife but the legitimate goal of marriage in the eyes of society. But this meant that people began expecting more of married life than ever before in history—at the exact time that older methods of organizing and stabilizing marriages were ceasing to work. The very things that made marriage more satisfying, and increasingly more fair to women, are the same things that have made marriage less stable.

Stephanie Coontz, *American Prospect*, April 8, 2002.

Even the most basic issue of self-definition creates problems when the language and categories available to us don't adequately describe unmarried lives. Every form seems to have checkboxes that ask us if we're married (no) or single (I certainly don't feel single). And one of the most common things unmarried couples wrestle with is what to call each other. Boyfriend and girlfriend sound too teenage; partner leads people to think you're business partners or gay; significant other is trying too hard; and spousal equivalent is just plain silly. Everyone in an unmarried relationship has had the experience of being introduced, "This is Margaret and her—uhh . . . mmmm . . . eh . . . *friend*."

The Future of Unmarriage

Projecting into the future based on the demographic trends of the last century and a half, the continuation of the gradual move away from marriage looks fairly inevitable. Writing in the *New York Times*, social commentator Katha Pollitt described the unlikely scenario that would have to take place to allow a return to mythologized Ozzie and Harriet families: "We'd have to restore the cult of virginity and the double standard, ban birth control, restrict divorce, kick women out of decent jobs, force unwed pregnant women to put their babies up for adoption on pain of social death, make out-of-wedlock children legal nonpersons. That's not going to happen."

The inescapable shift is taking place not just within our borders but also around the world. In the last decade marriage rates fell in Australia, Austria, Belgium, Bulgaria, China, France, Germany, Greece, Ireland, Israel, Italy, Portugal, Spain, Switzerland, and the UK, just to name a few. The percentage of births to unmarried parents rose in 14 of the 15 European Union countries, and is 39% or higher in a third of them. The number of unmarried parents in Japan grew 85% in the last five years, and in 2001 the Swiss marriage rate fell faster in a single year than it had in the previous eighty years. There's nothing to suggest people will quit the institution cold turkey. Instead, more will marry later or not at all; a significant portion of those who do marry won't stay together for life; people will marry for specific, practical reasons (childrearing, immigration, health benefits, etc.);

and acceptance of cohabitation will continue to increase.

It also seems clear that, eventually, the U.S. will give unmarried relationships and families social and legal standing comparable to that currently accorded to married ones. There's a lot to be learned by watching other countries grapple with unmarried relationships. Some, like Canada, France, and Sweden, have already overhauled their legal codes so that references to "spouse" also pertain to unmarried partners, or so that partners who meet certain criteria can register and gain "marital" rights as domestic partners. Others, like Australia, Belgium, Ireland, Mexico, New Zealand, Norway, South Africa, Uganda, and the UK have either taken initial steps toward broader recognition, or are currently engaged in national debates about how to best reconcile the gap between real families and those in the legal imaginary. Another set of nations is reacting to the changes entirely differently, as seen in news articles about women and couples in Nigeria and the United Arab Emirates who are sentenced to imprisonment, public floggings, or death by stoning for the crimes of cohabitation and unmarried sex. It does not seem presumptuous to assume that the U.S. will end up with a system more like Canada's than like Nigeria's.

Damage to Families

There are two questions that remain. First, how much damage will we do to children and families in the intervening time before we revise our social and legal codes? On a daily basis, unmarried people are denied access to health insurance, bi-national couples are prevented from being together, partners are shut out of hospital rooms, couples are shut out of faith communities, and people lose their homes when their partner dies without a will. Groups that oppose expanding rights to unmarried people and families base their arguments on the well-being of children and the strengthening of families. Yet their resistance functions to leave an ever-growing portion of American families out in the cold. The reality is stark: half of children today live in a family other than the one headed by their two married parents.

The second question is how the change will come about. Shifts in social support are likely to happen gradually on their own, as unmarried people and relationships become increasingly commonplace. But updating laws and policy is a more complex process. An organized grassroots lobby of unmarried people could bring change, like the War Widows of America who in the 1960s lobbied successfully to eliminate the "singles penalty" from the tax code. A high profile case of discrimination on the basis of marital status could turn legislators' sympathies, such as the scores of surviving partners of people killed on September 11, 2001, terrorist attacks who are currently denied access to most survivors' benefits. The lesbian, gay, bisexual, transgender rights movement has already succeeded in expanding recognition of diverse families in a myriad of ways, and is another likely leader in the movement for fairness.

Creating a Different Future

Social theorist Peter Drucker said, "The best way to predict the future is to create it." Lacking an obvious path to fair and equal treatment, those of us who recognize marital status as a social justice issue need to commit to making a difference where we can. Some of us can implement or agitate for workplace benefits policies that include employees' partners and dependents regardless of marital status. Some can create a culture of support and acceptance for diverse families in synagogues and churches, encourage unmarried people to take leadership positions, and offer relationship counseling in addition to marriage counseling. Some can strengthen unmarried couples' relationships by presiding over union or commitment ceremonies for those who seek a religious blessing but cannot or choose not to marry. Some can encourage legislators to expand the definition of family, so that families are recognized as people linked by emotional and financial care and interdependency, not limited to those connected by marriage, blood, or adoption.

All of us can become conscious of our language and assumptions. We can talk about partners along with spouses, pay attention to the word someone uses to identify his partner/ sweetheart/significant other, and make an effort to understand the meaning of a couple's own relationship rather than applying a one-size-fits-all model to everyone. We can learn more about the history and reality of marriage and families in the U.S. and around the world, to better understand the dangers of regressive policies that would "strengthen marriage" by increasing the privilege divide between married and unmarried. We can make contributions to the organizations—the Alternatives to Marriage Project, the Council on Contemporary Families, and others—that are on the front lines, who are regularly called on to debate spokespeople from groups with budgets hundreds of times larger than our own.

On a regular basis I still answer questions about why I'm not married, and I still argue with unenlightened rental car companies about why we should have to pay more than a married couple for a second driver. But I can also feel things shifting all around me. I receive my health insurance through the domestic partner policy at Marshall's workplace, and my doctor's office has a "partnered" checkbox on its patient forms. Recently, for our ninth anniversary, we got a card in the mail from my grandmother, which read, "Your commitment and love for each other is all that really counts. Hoping you keep celebrating to eternity!"

If the octogenarians get it, the rest of the country can't be far behind.

> *"Fatherlessness is cutting a swath of destruction through our nation that touches every American."*

Fathers Are Essential to Healthy Families

Alan W. Dowd

In the following viewpoint, Alan W. Dowd challenges a study by Louise Silverstein and Carl Auerbach that suggests that fathers may be unnecessary to a child's well-being. Dowd contends that fathers provide a unique role model that is essential to children's health. Dowd maintains that fatherless children do worse in school and engage in more criminal activity than children with fathers at home, and he concludes that government should do more to encourage fathers to accept their parental responsibilities. Dowd is a freelance writer and a former associate editor of the *American Legion* magazine.

As you read, consider the following questions:

1. As cited by Dowd, what are three conclusions about families reached by Silverstein and Auerbach?
2. What does the National Fatherhood Initiative suggest is today's most powerful cultural institution, as stated by the author?
3. What did Senator Bayh's Responsible Fatherhood Act of 2000 seek to develop, according to the author?

Hang up the baseball glove and put away the bedtime stories. No need to take that long walk with your daughter or have that long talk with your son. Keep the advice and hugs to yourself, and don't worry about coming home. If you're a father, you're no longer wanted or needed in 21st-century America.

This news may come as a shock, but it's just some of what Louise Silverstein and Carl Auerbach concluded in a jaw-dropping study on fathers and fatherhood aptly titled " Deconstructing the Essential Father." Published in *American Psychologist*, a journal of the American Psychological Association (APA), the study's radical conclusions further undermine what was once beyond debate—the idea that fathers play a crucial role in the health of families and children. Still sending shockwaves through public-policy circles more than a year after its initial publication, the study is just one of countless indicators that "Dad" is an endangered species.

Dangerous Dads?

Chipping away at some of our most basic conceptions of parenting, the APA study declares that fathers are not essential to child well-being; the institution of marriage does not serve the broader interests of society; divorce is not necessarily harmful to children; fathers contribute nothing special to child development; and the traditional family unit—headed by a mother and father—is not any better at protecting children than anything else. In other words, fathers are no longer relevant.

America's 25 million fatherless children might disagree. However, as Dr. Timothy Dailey, an analyst with the Family Research Council, uncovered in his cogent response to the APA study, Silverstein and Auerbach go beyond merely arguing that fathers are irrelevant: "The authors actually suggest that the traditional father can be harmful in the home," a flabbergasted Dailey explains.

In fact, in their view, "dear old Dad" is downright destructive and dangerous. Taking their counter-intuitive argument to the extreme, Silverstein and Auerbach contend that the traditional two-parent model of the family "fails to acknowledge the potential costs of father presence." According to Silverstein and Auerbach, many fathers do little more than waste family resources on gambling, alcohol and other vices.

Of course, fathers guilty of that kind of selfishness are out there, but they are the exception. Even so, it is that model of imperfection which seems to drive Silverstein and Auerbach's research. Given such a brutish and bleak picture of the typical father, it's easy to see why they arrive at their skewed conclusions.

Fathers on TV

But what would make them draw such a depressing caricature of the American father? A recent study by the National Fatherhood Initiative (NFI), a non-profit organization dedicated to increasing the number of children growing up with responsible fathers, has a possible answer: television.

"Today's most powerful cultural institution is television [and] children are its most ardent consumers," the NFI study begins. "Given the current scope of fatherlessness, it is no exaggeration to say that for millions of children the primary contact they have with the idea of a father is the time they spend watching a father on television."

Regrettably, what they usually see is similar to the distortion offered by Silverstein and Auerbach. The NFI study found that TV fathers are eight times more likely to be shown in a negative light than TV mothers. "On television," the study concludes, "fathers are less involved, provide less moral guidance, are less competent and place less of a priority on the family than do mothers."

NFI found that fully 65 percent of Hollywood's depictions of fatherhood provide either ambiguous or negative portrayals. In fact, 26 percent of the portrayals are completely negative. "This overabundance of 'bad dad' on television undermines a cultural ideal of responsible fatherhood at a time when that ideal is most needed," according to NFI's researchers.

Grim Numbers

From academia to pop culture, fatherhood is obviously under assault. What's happening to fathers and families is truly sobering. Indeed, the consequences of Dad's disappearance from America's family landscape illustrate how disconnected from reality Silverstein and Auerbach are.

Numbers and statistics sometimes distort the facts, but on rare occasions they truly illuminate. This is such an occasion.

Almost 25 million children live without fathers; 4 million don't even know who their fathers are; and 33 percent of the babies born in America today will be the sole responsibility of unmarried mothers.

Indeed, during the past three decades, fathers have disappeared from America faster than the spotted owl. According to the Family Research Council, 85 percent of all children lived in two-parent families in 1968. In 1980, it was 77 percent. Today, it's just 68 percent and falling. During those 30 years, the number of single-parent families in the United States quadrupled; the number of two-parent families inched up by just 8 percent.

This destabilizing trend of single-parenthood is continuing as we enter the 21st century. According to the Forum on Child and Family Statistics, a research arm of the federal government, birth rates have increased sharply for unmarried women in every age group during the past 20 years. And there's no evidence that what some have called "the epidemic of fatherlessness" will end.

Counting the Costs

This explosive increase in fatherless homes may seem irrelevant to traditional families or those who have already raised their children, but it isn't. In fact, it should send chills down their spines: Like a scythe, fatherlessness is cutting a swath of destruction through our nation that touches every American. Indeed, to look at these numbers is to look at the root cause of America's most intractable problems.

An ancient proverb warns, "When a father gives to his son, both laugh; when a son gives to his father, both cry." The children of absentee fathers are now paying back their parents and society for what they have been given—and deprived of—during the past 30 years. Their pain and anger are wreaking havoc with our country. And if we are not moved by their plight, we should at least be moved by self-interest. The longer the epidemic continues, the more profound and costly the consequences for every American.

According to Robert Maginnis, a specialist on fatherhood and family, fatherless kids are two times more likely to quit high school than those from two-parent families. They are 70 percent more likely to be kicked out of school, and 10 times more likely to abuse alcohol and other drugs.

Asay. © 1994 by Colorado Springs Gazette Telegraph. Reprinted by permission of Creators Syndicate, Inc.

The Forum on Child and Family Statistics found that children in one-parent households "are substantially more likely" to live in poverty. To be exact, they are five times more likely to live in poverty when compared to children lucky enough to be living with a mother and a father.

Fatherless Delinquents

But the consequences of Dad's disappearance aren't limited to economics or education. In most cases, the legacy of an absentee father is criminal behavior in his children.

"The likelihood that a young male will engage in criminal activity doubles if he is raised without a father," Maginnis said. No less than 72 percent of teen-age murderers grow up without a dad. And according to Cato Institute research, a

1-percent increase in births to single mothers triggers a 1.7-percent increase in violent crime. In fact, the Institute for Responsible Fatherhood and Family Revitalization has found that children from fatherless homes are 20 times more likely to end up in prison as their two-parent counterparts.

This should not be misunderstood as an attack on single mothers. Single moms are among the most creative and courageous people in America today. Working two and three jobs outside the home, they face the toughest job on earth inside the home alone. Many of their children grow up to be productive members of society. But the odds are against them. Most of their children will be forever scarred by Dad's absence and will pass the cycle of brokenness on to another generation. The old saying "like father, like son" is all too true.

Nor is this an endorsement of the misguided notion that any father—regardless of his behavior—is preferable to no father at all. The health and safety of a child or mother should never be sacrificed for the sake of a marriage. Indeed, it's better for some fathers to leave, but today one-third of them are walking away. That's far too many. Children grow up best when Mom and Dad raise them together. Ninety percent of single moms agree, and so do their kids, according to the Department of Health and Human Services.

Turning Point?

Thankfully, a handful of people and organizations are fighting for America's fathers and families. Were it not for them, there would be fewer of both.

Groups such as NFI, the Family Research Council, the Initiative for Responsible Fatherhood and Family Revitalization, and hundreds of other nonprofits are partnering with churches and public agencies to promote fatherhood and thereby protect mothers and their children from the long odds faced by fatherless homes. And their influence is being felt beyond the family room. After decades of indifference and outright contempt for fathers, the federal government is finally realizing the necessity of fathers and the value of two-parent families.

The examples abound—from the Department of Health and Human Services' Fatherhood Initiative to stronger child-support laws, from high-tech, interstate tracking of deadbeat dads to a wide array of pro-fatherhood legislation in Congress.

As Senator Evan Bayh, Democrat-Indiana, recently observed, "Addressing the problem of absent fathers must be a national priority because it impacts the well-being of America's children, families and communities." And since families are the building blocks of society, the epidemic of fatherlessness impacts the well-being of America itself.

Bayh's Responsible Fatherhood Act of 2000, which he co-wrote with Senator Pete Domenici, sought to develop an information clearinghouse to help states and agencies promote responsible fatherhood. The bill also would have reworked key aspects of the federal-state welfare system "to encourage the formulation and maintenance of two-parent families." However, the measure died in the Senate Finance Committee in 2000.

The Fathers Count Act proposed by Representative Nancy Johnson, Republican-Connecticut, would have provided grants to promote marriage and assist struggling fathers in job training. The bill also sought to ease some of the eligibility criteria on the Welfare-to-Work program. The bill passed the House with 328 votes. But it succumbed to the same fate as the Bayh-Domenici bill.

Congress clearly has plenty of ground to make up. Even so, perhaps the nation has reached a critical turning point. As NFI president Wade Horn notes, "Virtually everyone now agrees: Fathers matter."

Everyone, that is, except Hollywood and the APA.

"*We do not believe that the data support the conclusion that fathers are essential to child well-being.*"

Fathers Are Not Essential to Healthy Families

Louise B. Silverstein and Carl F. Auerbach

In the following viewpoint, Louise B. Silverstein and Carl F. Auerbach argue that traditional fathers may not be necessary to a child's well-being. They contend that children need stable, loving role models, and two parents are better than one, but they maintain that families do not have to adhere to the traditional father-plus-mother model for children to have positive outcomes. Silverstein and Auerbach challenge the neoconservative essentialist paradigm that asserts that men and women are biologically and culturally geared toward specific parental roles. They conclude that parenting duties are interchangeable, and that nontraditional households—such as single-parent, gay-parent, and step-parent—can successfully raise children. Silverstein and Auerbach are researchers at Yeshiva University in New York.

As you read, consider the following questions:
1. Why do the authors characterize the neoconservative perspective as "essentialist"?
2. According to the authors, how do marmosets challenge the neoconservative perspective?
3. What is the traditional father-child ideology, and how do the authors want to restructure it?

In the past two decades there has been an explosion of research on fathers. There is now a broad consensus that fathers are important contributors to both normal and abnormal child outcomes. Infants and toddlers can be as attached to fathers as they are to mothers. In addition, even when fathers are not physically present, they may play an important role in their children's psychological lives. Other important issues about fathers and families remain controversial. For example, scholars continue to debate the extent to which paternal involvement has increased over the past 20 years. Similarly, we are only beginning to study the ways that fathering identities vary across subcultures. Nor do we understand clearly the effects of divorce on fathers and their children.

Overall, this explosion of research on fathering has increased the complexity of scholarly thinking about parenting and child development. However, one group of social scientist has emerged that is offering a more simplistic view of the role of fathers in families. These neoconservative social scientists have replaced psychologist J. Bowlby's "essentializing" of mothers with a claim about the essential importance of fathers. These authors have proposed that the roots of a wide range of social problems (i.e. child poverty, urban decay, societal violence, teenage pregnancy, and poor school performance) can be traced to the absence of fathers in the lives of their children. . . . In our view, the essentialist framework represents a dramatic oversimplification of the complex relations between father presence and social problems.

The Essentialist Paradigm

We characterize this perspective as "essentialist" because it assumes that the biologically different reproductive functions of men and women automatically construct essential differences in parenting behaviors. The essentialist perspective defines mothering and fathering as distinct social roles that are not interchangeable. Marriage is seen as the social institution within which responsible fathering and positive child adjustment are most likely to occur. Fathers are understood as having a unique and essential role to play in child development, especially for boys who need a male role model in order to establish a masculine gender identity. . . .

In contrast to the neoconservative perspective, our data on gay fathering couples have convinced us that neither a mother nor a father is essential. Similarly, our research with divorced, never-married, and remarried fathers has taught us that a wide variety of family structures can support positive child outcomes. We have concluded that children need at least one responsible, caretaking adult who has a positive emotional connection to them, and with whom they have a consistent relationship. Because of the emotional and practical stress involved in childrearing, a family structure that includes more than one such adult is more likely to contribute to positive child outcomes. Neither the sex of the adult(s), nor the biological relationship to the child has emerged as a significant variable in predicting positive development. One, none, or both of those adults could be a father [or mother]. We have found that the stability of the emotional connection and the predictability of the caretaking relationship are the significant variables that predict positive child adjustment.

We agree with the neoconservative perspective that it is preferable for responsible fathers [and mothers] to be actively involved with their children. We share the concern that many men in U.S. society do not have a feeling of emotional connection or a sense of responsibility toward their children. However, we do not believe that the data support the conclusion that fathers are essential to child well-being, and that heterosexual marriage is the only social context in which responsible fathering is most likely to occur.

Many social scientists believe that it is possible to draw a sharp distinction between scientific fact and political values. From our perspective, science is always structured by values, both in the research questions that are generated, and in the interpretation of data. For example, if one considers the heterosexual nuclear family to be the optimal family structure for child development, then one is likely to design research that looks for negative consequences associated with growing up in a gay or lesbian parented family. If, in contrast, one assumes that gay and lesbian parents can create a positive family context, then one is likely to initiate research that investigates the strengths of children raised in these families.

Essentialist Legislation

The essentialist theoretical framework has already generated a series of social policy initiatives. For example, a 1998 Congressional seminar that recommended a series of revisions [which were not made] to the tax code that would: reward couples who marry; and end taxes altogether for married couples with three or more children. Other federal legislation has emerged with a similar emphasis on the advantages of marriage. The 1996 welfare reform law begins by stating, "Marriage is the foundation of a successful society." Similarly, a housing project in Hartford, Connecticut now provides economic supports to married couples, and special opportunities for job training to men (but not to women) who live with their families. In 1997, Louisiana passed a Covenant Marriage Act that declared marriage a lifelong relationship, and stipulated more stringent requirements for separation and divorce. . . .

Specific aspects of the neoconservative paradigm have been critiqued elsewhere. For example, V.C. McLoyd, in his article "Socioeconomic Disadvantage and Child Development," has pointed out that families without fathers are likely to be poor; and it is the negative effects of poverty, rather than the absence of a father, that lead to negative developmental outcomes. Similarly, pschologists E.M. Hetherington, M. Bridges, and G.M. Insabella have made the point that divorce does not always have negative consequences for children. However, the neoconservative argument as a whole has not been deconstructed. Thus, it tends to be absorbed in a monolithic fashion, buttressed by unconscious gender ideology and traditional cultural values. Therefore, we think that a systematic counterargument is necessary. . . .

Biological Sex Differences

One of the cornerstones of the essentialist position is that biological differences in reproduction construct gender differences in parenting behaviors. This theoretical framework proposes that the biological experiences of pregnancy and lactation generate a strong, instinctual drive in women to nurture. This perspective assumes that men do not have an instinctual drive to nurture infants and children.

The neoconservative perspective relies heavily on evolutionary psychology to support this argument. Evolutionary psychologists cite R.L. Trivers' sexual conflict of interest hypothesis to explain sex differences in mating strategies. Trivers' hypothesis states that, all other things being equal, male mammals will maximize their evolutionary fitness by impregnating as many females as possible, while investing very little in the rearing of any individual offspring. Female mammals, in contrast, invest a great deal of physiological energy in pregnancy and lactation, and thus are motivated to invest a corresponding amount of time and energy in parenting. . . .

David Blankenhorn, author of *Fatherless America: Confronting Our Most Urgent Social Problem*, and David Popenoe, co-founder of the National Marriage Project, like many social scientists, have incorrectly assumed that Trivers' theory is true of all primates, and universally applicable across many different ecological contexts. However, all other things have generally not been equal over the course of evolutionary history. As bioecological contexts change, so do fathering behaviors, especially among primate males.

Marmosets are an extreme example of primates who live in a bioecological context that requires males to become primary caretakers. Because marmosets always have twins, female marmosets must nurse two infants simultaneously. This generates nutritional pressure for the mother to spend all of her time and energy feeding herself. Therefore the father most commonly performs all parenting behaviors. Thus, these animals do not conform to Trivers' hypothesis about the universality of non-nurturing primate males. Marmoset males behave like "full-time mothers.". . .

Another cornerstone of the essentialist position is that the traditional division of labor characteristic of Western, industrialized societies has been true throughout human evolutionary history. Popenoe stated that our hominid ancestors "had a strong division of labor in which males did most of the hunting and females did most of the gathering." A.L. Zihlman, in her essay "Women's Bodies, Women's Lives: An Evolutionary Perspective," in contrast, has pointed out that for most of our evolutionary history, human societies were nomadic. This bioecological context required both men and

The Essentialist Paradigm

1. Biological Sex Differences Construct Gender Differences in Parenting.

   The biological experiences of pregnancy and lactation generate a strong, instinctual drive in women to nurture. In the absence of these experiences, men do not have an instinctual drive to nurture infants and children.

2. The Civilizing Effects of Marriage.

   a. Because a man's contribution to reproduction is limited to the moment of conception, active and consistent parenting on the part of men is universally difficult to achieve.

   b. The best way to insure that men will consistently provide for and nurture young children is to provide a social structure in which men can be assured of the paternity, i.e. the traditional nuclear family. Without the social institution of marriage, men are likely to impregnate as many women as possible, without behaving responsibly to their offspring.

3. The importance of a male role model.

   If men can be induced to caretake young children, their unique, masculine contribution significantly improves developmental outcomes for children. This is especially true for boys who need a male role model in order to achieve a psychologically healthy masculine gender identity.

Louise B. Silverstein and Carl F. Auerbach, *American Psychologist*, June 1999.

---

women to travel long distances, hunt, gather food, and care for older children and other members of their community. Similarly, in contemporary foraging and horticultural societies, women perform the same range of tasks as men do, and add infant care to their other responsibilities. Cross-cultural research illustrates that women are capable of traveling long distances, carrying heavy loads, and participating in hunting. Thus, the assertion that a rigid sexual division of labor existed over most of our evolutionary history is not supported, either by what is known about human society in prehistory, or by contemporary preagricultural cultures. . . .

The Civilizing Effects of Marriage

The essentialist position has also proposed that marriage has a "civilizing" effect on men. Popenoe, reflecting this point of view, has stated that ". . . all successful societies have imposed social sanctions on men . . . the most important of these is the institution of marriage." Similarly, Blankenhorn declared that "marriage constitutes an irreplaceable life support system for effective fatherhood."

Blankenhorn further asserted that marriage protects women and children from domestic violence. He reported that, as the percentage of men living within the confines of marriage has declined over the past two decades, domestic violence has increased. However, a 1998 report on intimate violence published by the U.S. Department of Justice indicated that, as marriage has declined over the past two decades, so has intimate violence. This report stated that murders of women by their intimate partners decreased 40%, from 3,000 in 1976, to 1800 in 1996. Similarly, nonlethal violence (sexual assault, robbery, aggravated and simple assault), declined from 1.1 million reported incidents in 1993, to 840,000 in 1996. . . .

The Importance of a Male Role Model

Another aspect of the neoconservative perspective is the argument that "key parental tasks belong essentially and primarily to fathers," according to Blankenhorn. Fathers are seen as essential role models for boys, relationship models for girls, and "protectors" of their families, as stated by Popenoe. However, there is a considerable body of empirical evidence that contradicts these claims.

The essentialist perspective assumes that boys need a heterosexual male parent in order to establish a masculine gender identity. J.H. Pleck, in his essay "The Gender Role Strain: An Update," has demonstrated that empirical research does not support this assumption. Similarly, a significant amount of research on the children of lesbian and gay parents has shown that children raised by lesbian mothers (and gay fathers) are as likely as children raised in a heterosexual, two-parent family to achieve a heterosexual gender orientation. Other aspects of personal development and social relationships were also found to be within the normal range for children raised in lesbian and gay families.

However, persistent, although inconsistent, findings suggest that the negative impact of divorce is more significant for boys than girls. After reviewing the divorce and remarriage research, E.M. Hetherington, M. Bridges, and G.M. Insabella concluded that "the presence of a father may have positive effects on the well-being of boys." These authors also pointed out that the research is not clear as to how father presence acts as a protective factor for boys. H. Lytton and D.M. Romney in a meta-analysis of 172 studies found very few significant differences in the ways that mothers and fathers treated girls and boys. Similarly M.E. Lamb concluded that "very little about the gender of the parent seems to be distinctly important," in his essay "Fathers and Child Development: An Introductory Overview and Guide." Thus, the relation between father presence and better developmental outcomes for boys remains correlational, not causal.

Social Changes

If the essentialist paradigm is not supported by empirical data, why has it been so widely accepted? We believe that the appeal of the essentialist position reflects a reaction against the rapid changes in family life that have taken place in the past three decades. Since the 1960's, family formation strategies have changed dramatically in Western, industrialized cultures. The cultural norm of early and universal marriage has been reversed. Fertility rates have declined overall, and age at the birth of a first child has risen across all cohorts. More couples are choosing to live together outside the context of marriage, and a first pregnancy more frequently precedes, rather than follows marriage. Previously rare family types, e.g. single-mothers-by-choice, dual career, and gay/lesbian-parents are increasingly more common.

Industrialized cultures are in the process of changing from a context in which child development could flourish with fathers as the sole or primary provider, to a context in which two providers are now necessary in the vast majority of families. In a survey of 1,502 U.S. families, 48% of married women reported that they provided half or more of the family income. Given this commitment to breadwinning, women can no longer shoulder the sole responsibility for raising children.

In this context of rapid change, the neoconservative position reflects a widespread societal anxiety about "Who will raise the children?" Mothers are no longer at home, and society has not embraced "other-than-mother" care. The U.S., in contrast to other western countries, has not yet developed a social policy agenda designed to help women and men integrate their work and family responsibilities. Thus, many people believe that a return to the traditional nuclear family structure with its gendered division of labor would be preferable to large numbers of neglected and unsupervised children. . . .

An Alternative Blueprint for Social Change

Because we believe that ideology defines both social policy and individual behavior, our first recommendation speaks to the necessity of reconstructing cultural ideology about gender roles. The neoconservative perspective also wants to reconnect fatherhood and masculinity. Blankenhorn has stated that "being a real man [must come to mean] being a good father." However, within the essentialist framework, responsible fathering is inextricably intertwined with marriage. Our goal, in contrast, is to create an ideology that defines the father-child bond as independent of the father-mother relationship.

If the father-child bond were accorded the same importance as the mother-child bond, then young boys would be socialized to assume equal responsibility for the care and nurturing of their children. A father's relationship with his children could then develop and remain independent of his relationship with the child's mother. This ideological shift would encourage the development of diverse models of responsible fatherhood. . . .

We believe that this change in cultural gender ideology would be effective in maintaining a high level of paternal involvement for resident as well as nonresident fathers. Divorce and nonmarital childbirth would then be less likely to be characterized by father absence, since cultural norms would prescribe that never-married and divorced fathers remain actively involved with their children.

This ideological enhancement of the father-child bond is also necessary for restructuring societal institutions so that father involvement is encouraged, rather than inhibited. Maintaining the sacred status of the mother-child dyad continues the myth of separate, i.e. gendered, spheres of life. The cultural assumption of separate spheres links public/work/masculine and private/family/feminine. This cultural linking of family and feminine is reflected in the assumption that women, but not men, will decrease their involvement in paid work in order to balance the competing demands of work and family life. . . .

Restructuring Family Policy

Our final recommendation relates to an overall governmental family policy. The U.S. cultural ideology of rugged individualism continues to assume that individual families can and should balance the stress of work and family without the benefits of large-scale government supports. The U.S. remains one of the few industrialized countries without a comprehensive family policy that provides: paid parental leave, governmentally financed day care, and economic subsidies for all families with children. Without these benefits, the responsibility for childcare continues to fall largely on women.

Because women continue to bear the bulk of the responsibility for the welfare of children, the goal of economic equality remains elusive. Providing families with governmental supports would not only alleviate many of the stresses of working families, it would also free women from the unequal burden of making major accommodations in their involvement in paid work. This shift would then decrease gender inequalities in the workplace, provide women with more resources to exchange, and thus contribute to higher paternal involvement. . . .

We have tried to illustrate how the essentialist position does not accurately reflect relevant empirical research. We have provided an alternative explanation of the research, and generated recommendations for social policy supports to mothers and fathers that we believe will more effectively achieve the goal of reconnecting fathers and children. We hope that this article will generate scholarly debate within the psychological community, and encourage a critical analysis of the essentialist paradigm.

| "In real marriages, male headship is simply a fact."

Traditional Husband and Wife Roles Help Maintain Healthy Families

Steven E. Rhoads

According to Steven E. Rhoads in the following viewpoint, men and women have biologically prescribed behaviors that complement each other in marriage. Rhoads argues that marriages flourish when men are dominant breadwinners and females are homemakers. He contends that while males are biologically and culturally suited to exercise power, women are suited to nurturing children. Rhoads is a professor of government at the University of Virginia.

As you read, consider the following questions:
1. According to Rhoads, why are feminists disgusted by married men?
2. As cited by the author, how do men and women define equality in marriage?
3. How can men be convinced to dominate less in marriage, according to the author?

Steven E. Rhoads, "The Case Against Androgynous Marriage," *American Enterprise*, Vol. 10, September 1999, pp. 35–39. Copyright © 1999 by American Enterprise Institute for Public Policy Research. Reproduced with permission.

Candace Bergen has now admitted what her TV character, Murphy Brown, never did: Fathers matter. Social scientists have never been more sure, because fathers help boys become responsible men and teach girls good men will love them even if they don't "put out."

And when men—even men who have been good fathers—divorce their wives, they usually end up divorcing their children as well. Two leading family experts, Frank Furstenberg and Andrew Cherlin, find that "over time, the vast majority of children [of divorce] will have little or no contact with their fathers." So if we care about the future of our kids, we should care about finding the secrets to marriages that last through "sickness and health," through "better and worse."

Traditional Christian Marriages

These traditional phrases from church weddings might remind one of the traditional Christian understanding of marriage—one where wives "submit" to the "servant" leadership of their husbands. In 1999 the Southern Baptists reminded the faithful of this Biblical teaching, and feminists denounced it as "domestic feudalism."

Most of the rest of America shrugged it off. After all, androgyny is everywhere. Women fly jets and make up 43 percent of all law school graduates. Men go to hair stylists and wear earrings. To most of us, male headship seems like something from another planet.

But social science research on intact marriages finds that in real marriages, male headship is simply a fact. Most men and women seek things in a mate that render something like male headship inevitable. If we care about marriages that work, the Baptists just may have something to teach us.

Feminists can hardly look at married men without a certain measure of disgust. Men won't do their share of housework and child care. In the typical two-earner family they contribute about half as much housework as their employed wives and less than half as much solo child care.

Most feminists believe men's power in the home comes from their power in the marketplace. In *Ms. Magazine* one family therapist sets forth her golden rule of marriage, "Whoever has the gold makes the rules." But the overworked wives cited above are already bringing home gold. Perhaps they're not bringing home enough? To answer, we need to know whether women's power soars when they are the big earners in marriage.

Women as Breadwinners

When husbands make more than wives, both say the husband's job is the more important, but when wives earn more, neither spouse says the wife's job is more important. Indeed, such wives are more likely than other married women to leave the labor force or move to a lower position. At home these high-achieving wives attempt to be especially attractive and sexual for their husbands, and they report indulging husbands' whims and salving egos. When husbands are more dependent on their wives' incomes, the husbands do very little additional housework.

Questions of income aside, there are, of course, marriages where women have more power. Do such marriages make women happy? One survey of over 20 studies on marital power found that wife-dominant couples were the least happy, and the wives in wife-dominated unions were less happy than their husbands.

Researcher Liz Gallese's study of women graduates from the 1975 class of the Harvard Business School finds that the women have a tendency to "pull back" on their way to the top. One woman who did not do so was Tess. When her career shot past her husband's, he took on most of the child care. On the surface Tess's marriage made role reversal look workable. Tess seemed proud of her job, her son, and her husband. Gallese did not glimpse the truth until she spent time alone with Tess's husband, who admitted he and his wife had almost no sex life, though he would try to "do things to rekindle her interest."

Soon Tess began to seduce other businessmen. Eventually she came clean with Gallese, admitting that she would love to have another child someday but not with her husband. She stayed with him because he was "a wife." "I absolutely refuse to sleep with that man. I'll never have sex with him again."

Feminists will no doubt say they want neither an old-fashioned marriage nor Tess's but rather one in which promotions and relocations come in tandem or sequentially. But

Bible Rules for a Happy Marriage

Colossians 3:18 and 19 says: "Wives, be subject to your husbands, as is fitting in the Lord. Husbands, love your wives, and do not be embittered against them." What is notable in our day about these simple commands of the Apostle is that they differentiate between the role and duty of the wife and the role and duty of the husband. . . .

If a husband is blessed with an intelligent, well-educated, and competent wife, it will be that husband's greatest wisdom to encourage his wife to use those gifts to the fullest as his wife. A wife must remember, however, that those gifts are not to be used to advance her own independent career path, but to support and advance her husband and their home. Those gifts come from God. They are to be used for God and used in fulfillment of the role He has given to her as a wife.

If God gives a man a suitable helper in the Lord, that man should make it his highest goal to be the head to her he should be. As her leader and head, he must love her. All that he does must be consistent with her highest and best interests. He should never make an important decision without consulting her. He should always seek her best interests.

Samuel E. Waldron, "Bible Rules for a Happy Marriage," April 2000.

---

marriages in which spouses devote equal time to work, home, and children are very rare, and rarer still are marriages in which the spouses are equally successful in all realms. Researcher Pepper Schwartz searched hard to find couples where there was at least a 60/40 split of duties on the home front. Her study found that such "peer" couples feel they have a strong marital relationship with intimacy, mutual respect, and mutual interest. But they also face serious problems. Many husbands are unhappy when their careers suffer. There are constant negotiations and compromises, and serious conflicts over child rearing. . . .

The Appeal of Male Power

Ordinary women show the attractions of male power by making the romance novel the most popular form of fiction in the world. About half of all mass market paperback sales in the country are romance novels. The hero in the romance novel is always a man with power; the heroine seldom has worldly power.

In real life, most women do not seem to want equal worldly power. Even professional women want the man to be chief provider, not only because they believe the husband's work is more important to his sense of self, but also because they need their husbands to be successful.

For feminists the news gets worse. Working women say they respect stay-at-home moms more than mothers who work full time. When asked whether the increased number of working mothers with young children is good or bad for society, women of all educational levels think it is bad, and college-educated women are particularly likely to think so.

Finally, most women with full-time jobs do not resent their double shift. Despite the imbalance in housework and child care, the majority of wives think the division of labor is fair. Husbands and wives tend to define equality in marriage as mutual respect, commitment, and reciprocity over time, rather than as an equal division of tasks.

The Marital Ideal

Once we look at what is known of men's and women's natures, it's not surprising women take to domestic life more readily. It may seem remarkable that men marry at all. The marital ideal is about one man and one woman becoming bound in body and soul—sharing, comforting, communicating through good times and bad. But this ideal resonates more strongly for women than for men. Men want more space. Studies show women like to be alone by thinking in a bedroom or office, whereas men are more likely to need real isolation—a long drive or a trip to the mountains. Think also of those frequently solitary and overwhelmingly male pastimes, hunting and fishing.

Feminists such as Deborah Tannen and Carol Gilligan make much of the male insistence on standing alone. They think society conditions men to be this way. Theresa Crenshaw, co-author of a leading medical text on sexual pharmacology, once agreed but now thinks the source is testosterone: "The 'loner profile' of testosterone is absolutely crucial to understanding what men are all about. . . . Testosterone motivates the male to strive for separateness in ways a woman is not designed to comprehend." Indeed, "It is fair to say that it causes a compelling sexual urge that spurns relationships, unless they represent a conquest or acquisition of power. . . . It makes you want sex, but it also makes you want to be alone, or thoroughly in control of sexual situations—so it specifically promotes masturbation or one-night stands."

Female sexuality usually functions as a means of expressing affection to someone in a committed relationship. Women's sexual fantasies dwell more on romance, commitment, nonsexual caressing, and story line. . . .

The androgyny advocates believe that with different social conditioning, men can be reprogrammed to become fully intimate, communicative partners like their wives. And once reprogrammed, men will gain from the sharing of problems as women do. But the testosterone research suggests otherwise. So too does a study that followed the progress of patients dismissed from hospitals after recovery from congestive heart failure. For women the absence of emotional support in the community increased their death rates more than eightfold. For men it made no difference at all. . . .

Women as Nurturers

The average woman's innate attachment to and skill with babies would, by itself, be more than enough to sink the androgyny project since most men cannot match women in either the attachment or the skill. Mothers everywhere, in all cultures, take care of young children. This seems to be true even in alternative family forms such as communal living groups and unmarried couples.

Feminists talk a lot about the "burdens" of child care and the "sacrifices" that women make for it. Some women do find child care boring and depressing. But most do not. In her powerful defense of homemakers, *Domestic Tranquility*, Carolyn Graglia describes her child-rearing days as an "everyday epiphany of exquisite happiness." Award-winning novelist Alice McDermott sounded the same note in describing how she and her graduate school classmates were transformed by motherhood. The joy of children seemed "too satisfying, too marvelous" to be put in words. But they tried: "Becoming a mother is the best thing I've ever done." "It's like floating in warm milk." "I could fill a stadium with babies.". . .

Women's estrogen facilitates the effect of oxytocin, a substance which promotes touching, holding, and bonding. During pregnancy and nursing oxytocin surges in women, engendering pleasure and relaxation. When male rats are given oxytocin, they start building nests like their sisters.

The effect of male hormones on nurturing is dramatically different. Evidence comes from studies of women exposed to high levels of male hormones in their mothers' wombs. These women have little interest in dolls as children, and compared to most women, they are less attracted to infants as adults. On the other hand, Turner's syndrome girls, who do not produce the small amount of male hormone most women do, show heightened interest in dolls and babies.

Women's keener sense of touch makes them more responsive to babies, and their high, sing-song voices have been shown to be more pleasing than men's attempts at baby talk. Especially pleasing is a mother's voice. Babies hear it in utero, and after birth its sound slows, calms, and steadies a baby's heart.

Given women's greater interest in and skill with young children, it is fortunate that the vast majority of women and men think wives should concentrate on nurturing and husbands on providing. Data on the proportions of husbands and wives who work full time does not accurately reflect husbands' greater commitment to the work force. Sixty-one percent of husbands work more than 40 hours a week, whereas only 24 percent of wives do. Moreover, husbands are seven times more likely to work more than 60 hours a week. And though 51 percent of wives with children under 18 work full time, only 30 percent want to.

Different Reasons for Divorce

These figures do not point to an androgynous future, and if we want strong marriages we should be delighted. The richest discussion of American men and women's reasons for divorce, Catherine Riessman's *Divorce Talk*, finds women divorcing men who do not work steadily at good jobs; in parallel fashion men divorce women when they fall down as homemakers. Philip Blumstein and Pepper Schwartz's major work, *American Couples*, finds exactly the same thing. Women are much more likely to divorce men who are not ambitious, whereas men are more likely to divorce women who are ambitious. Men divorce wives if they think the wives are not doing their share of the housework. Women do not divorce men if the men do less housework than they would like them to. . . .

In marriage men and women get exactly what they want. If you ask men how they would like to be described, they use words like "dominant," "assertive," "independent." If you ask women how they would like to be described, they say "loving," "generous," "sensitive." But if marriage means bringing together one person with a taste for domination and another with a taste for generosity, we should not be surprised to find that the former is the head of the family.

In marriages women are more accommodating. If husbands think it is important to have a "proper" dinner, again, it is the wives who spend more time on housework. In family quarrels during dinner, mothers are most likely to compromise. Daughters are the next most likely to. Theresa Crenshaw thinks these inclinations go deep: One reason "women are the peacemakers" is their hormonal makeup. "Mellowing them are their relatively high levels of serotonin compared to the male, oxytocin in abundant supply, and estrogen, a gentle, ordinarily soothing antidepressant hormone."

Another reason women are the peacemakers is their deep need for amiable connection. And their most important connections are at home. Women say that family relationships are the key to their happiness. Family distress has more effect on the mental health of wives than of husbands. For husbands, satisfaction in work or as a parent can offset an unhappy marriage. But for wives, feminist Rosalind Barnett and coauthors report that "dissatisfaction in the marital role cannot be compensated for by satisfaction in any other role.". . .

Tempering Male Headship

If any women should still be reading, please note I have been describing how things are. As for how things might be, I would argue for a kinder and gentler male headship. For all the reasons given, the headship part won't go away. Most women don't really want it to. They like a manly man in the outside world and in the bedroom. They could, however, do with men who are a little less lordly in the rest of the house.

And if we care about solid marriages that rear solid children, we have to side with wives here. Riessman's *Divorce Talk* describes women filing for divorce because they feel devalued and dominated. In retrospect even their former husbands often agree they were treating their wives like "a dictator" or "a little Hitler." Although many happy marriages are characterized by moderate male dominance, marriages often fail when there is extreme male dominance. Researcher John Gottman finds successful marriages have a husband who accepts a wife's influence. They also have wives who couch complaints in a gentle, soothing, sometimes humorous way.

But how can we induce the stronger sex that likes to dominate to do it less? This is where the Baptists can help, by reminding men of their sacred obligation to use their familial power to serve their families. Husbands must be ready to sacrifice themselves for their wives and children as Christ gave all for the church. By making the male role in marriage vital, Baptists attract more men to it. And by condemning extramarital sex, they make alternatives to marriage less attractive and less available. . . .

Wives doubtful about granting husbands titular headship should realize they may not have to give up much more than the title. Studies suggest husbands overestimate their decision-making power while wives underestimate theirs. Indeed, one study found "the most satisfied husbands were those who believed they had the greater decision-making power even where there was no independent evidence of it."

Women in such marriages probably rule indirectly as the wisest wives usually do. Author David Blankenhorn tells the tale of a traditional wife who said her husband was the head of the family and she was the neck—which turns the head in the direction it should go. Most wives set husbands going in better directions, and civilization is in their debt.

"Gendered marriages . . . do not fit with the assumptions about men and women in all other spheres of their lives."

Traditional Husband and Wife Roles Must Change

Steven L. Nock

In the following viewpoint, Steven L. Nock argues that women have made enormous gains in social and workplace equality since the 1960s. These changes brought enormous benefits to women but undermined the traditional family because marital roles failed to change with external roles. For example, many marriages are stressed because most women work full time just as their husbands do, but men do not share equally in the housework. Nock concludes that modern marriages must revise the traditional family model to fit new social realities. Nock is a sociology professor at the University of Virginia and the author of *Marriage in Men's Lives*.

As you read, consider the following questions:

1. How does the author define the traditional marriage model?
2. What does Nock contend are the six ideals of legal marriage?
3. What aspect of the normative model of marriage would change with a new model of marriage, according to the author?

Steven L. Nock, "The Problem With Marriage," *Society*, Vol. 36, July/August 1999, pp. 20–28. Copyright © 1999 by Transaction Publishers, Inc. Reproduced with permission.

S table marriages are forged of extensive dependencies. Yet trends toward gender equality and independence have made the traditional basis of economic dependency in marriage increasingly problematic. The challenge is to reinvent marriage as an institution based on dependency that is not automatically related to gender. Both partners, that is, must gain significantly from their union, and both must face high exit costs for ending it.

Despite dramatic changes in law and public policy that have erased (or minimized) distinctions between men and women, married life has changed more slowly and subtly. In the last four decades, the percentage of married women in the paid labor force increased from 32 percent to 59 percent, and the number of hours that wives commit to paid labor increased apace. While men do not appear to be doing much more housework today than they did two decades ago, women are doing less in response to their commitments to paid labor. Women did 2.5 times as much household labor as their husbands in 1975. By 1987, the ratio was 1.9. Wives' share of total (reported) household income increased marginally, from 35 percent in 1975–1980 to 38 percent in 1986–1991. In such small ways, husbands and wives are increasingly similar. Still, marriages are hardly genderless arrangements. My research for *Marriage in Men's Lives* showed that most marriages in America resemble a traditional model, with husbands as heads of households, and wives who do most housework and child care. Given the pace at which gender distinctions have been, or are being, eliminated from laws, work, school, religion, politics, and other institutions, the family appears to be curiously out of step.

Marriage Defines Gender Roles

One reason gender is still a central motif in marriage is because masculinity (and possibly, femininity) are defined by, and displayed in marriage. As the title of Sara Berk's book proclaimed, the family is *The Gender Factory*. Consider the consequences of unemployment for husbands. If spouses were economically rational, then the unemployed (or lower-paid) partner would assume responsibility for housework. Sociologist Julie Brines found just the opposite. After a few months of unemployment, husbands actually reduced their housework efforts. The reason is that housework is much more than an economic matter. It is also symbolic. "Men's" work means providing for the family and being a "breadwinner," whereas "women's" work means caring for the home and children. Such assumptions are part of our cultural beliefs. Doing housework, earning a living, providing for the family, and caring for children are ways of demonstrating masculinity or femininity. When wives are economically dependent on their husbands, doing housework is consistent with traditional assumptions about marriage. Such women conform to cultural understandings about what it means to be a wife, or a woman. However, a dependent husband departs from customary assumptions about marriage and men. Were he to respond by doing more housework, his deviance would be even greater. Marriage is still the venue in which masculinity and femininity are displayed.

The husband and wife who construct a new model of marriage that doesn't include gender as a primary organizing principle will face challenges. The husband who decides to be the primary child-care provider or the wife who elects to be the sole wage earner will find these unusual marital roles difficult but not impossible to sustain. Relationships with parents may be awkward. Friends may struggle to understand the arrangement if it differs from their own. Employers may also find such an arrangement difficult to understand and accept. Yet as difficult as it may be to forge a new model of marriage, it seems certain that some change is necessary if marriage is to endure. . . .

Different Lives, Different Marriages

Research confirms that most women who marry today desire marriages that differ importantly from those of their grandmothers because women's lives have changed in so many other ways in recent decades. However, though the options available to women have expanded in other respects, the basic pattern of marriage is pretty much the same as it has been for decades. The revolution in gender has not yet touched women's marriages. Part of the reason is that men have been excluded from the gender revolution. While almost any young woman today will notice enormous differences between her life options and those of her great-grandmother, the differences between men and their great-grandfathers are minimal, at most. The script for men in America has not changed. In short, despite enormous changes in what it means to be a woman, marriage does not yet incorporate those changes. Neither men nor women have yet figured out how to fashion "new" families.

Many of our problems are better seen as the result of institutional change than of individual moral decline. The personal problems that lead to family decline are also legitimate public issues. Institutions like the family are bigger than any individual. So when large numbers of people create new patterns of family life, we should consider the collective forces behind such novel arrangements. And if some of those innovations are harmful to adults or children, fixing them will require more than a call for stronger moral habits (though there is certainly nothing wrong with such advice). Fixing them will require restructuring some basic social arrangements. . . .

The Institution of Marriage

The extent to which the family based on legal marriage is an institution becomes obvious when one considers an alternative way that adult couples arrange their intimate lives. Certainly there is no reason to believe that two people cannot enjoy a harmonious and happy life without the benefit of legal marriage. In fact, growing numbers of Americans appear to believe that unmarried cohabitation offers something that marriage does not. One thing that cohabitation offers is freedom from the rules of marriage because there are no widely accepted and approved boundaries around cohabitation. Unmarried partners have tremendous freedom to decide how they will arrange their legal and other relationships. Each partner must decide how to deal with the other's parents, for example. Parents, in turn, may define a cohabiting child's relationship as different from a married child's. Couples must decide whether vacations will be taken together or separately. Money may be pooled or held in separate accounts. If children are born, cohabiting parents must decide about the appropriate (non-legal) obligations each incurred as a result. In such small ways, cohabiting couples and their associates must create a relationship. Married couples may also face decisions about some of these matters. However, married spouses have a pattern to follow. For most matters of domestic life, marriage supplies a template. This is what cohabiting couples lack. They are exempt from the vast range of marriage norms and laws in our society. . . .

Almost all worrisome social trends in regard to the family are actually problems related to marriage: declining rates of marriage, non-marital fertility, unmarried cohabitation, and divorce. Any understanding of the family must begin with a consideration of marriage. I now offer a normative definition of marriage; a statement of what Americans agree it should be, the assumptions and taken-for-granted notions involved. In so doing, I will lay the foundation for an explanation of family decline. . . .

A normative definition of marriage draws attention to the central idea that marriage is more than the sum of two spouses. As an institution, marriage includes rules that originate outside the particular union that establish boundaries around the relationship. Those boundaries are the understood limits of behavior that distinguish marriage from all other relationships. Married couples have something that all other couples lack; they are heirs to a system of shared principles that help organize their lives. If we want to assess changes in the family, the starting point is an examination of the institutional foundation of marriage. Six ideals define legal marriage in America.

1. Individual Free Choice. Mate selection is based on romantic love. . . . National surveys show that "falling in love" is the most frequently cited reason for marrying one's spouse, and that the most important traits in successful marriages are thought to be "satisfying one another's needs" and "being deeply in love."

2. Maturity. Domestic relations law defines an age at which persons may marry. Throughout the U.S., the minimum is 18, though marriage may be permitted with approval by parents or the court at earlier ages. . . .

3. Heterosexuality. . . . Despite growing acceptance of homosexuality, there is very little support for homosexual

marriages. The 1990 General Social Survey showed that only 12 percent of Americans believe homosexuals should be allowed to marry.

4. Husband as Head. Though Americans generally endorse equality between the sexes, men and women still occupy different roles in their marriages. Even if more and more couples are interested in egalitarian marriages, large numbers of people aren't. The 1994 General Social Survey shows that adults are almost evenly divided about whether both spouses should contribute to family income (57 percent approve of wives working, and in fact, 61 percent of wives are employed). Four in ten adults endorse a very traditional division of roles, where the wife takes care of the home and family, and the husband earns all the income. . . .

5. Fidelity and Monogamy. In law, sexual exclusivity is the symbolic core of marriage, defining it in more obvious ways than any other. Husbands and wives have a legal right to engage in (consensual) sex with one another. Other people may not have a legal right to engage in sex with either married partner. . . .

6. Parenthood. With rare exceptions, married people become parents. Despite high rates of unmarried fertility, there is little to suggest that married couples are less likely to have, or desire to have children today than they were several decades ago. Only 13 percent of ever-married women aged 34 to 45 are childless today. Two decades ago, the comparable figure was 7 percent. The six-point difference, however, is due to delayed fertility, rather than higher childlessness. Overall completed cohort fertility (i.e., the total number of children born to women in their lifetime) has remained stable since the end of the Baby Boom. . . .

New Families

It is easy to imagine how a new model of marriage would look. None of the basic elements of normative marriage are likely to change except the gender assumptions about who heads the family. Husbands and wives are already familiar with this new model of marriage, even if we have yet to acknowledge it. In 1995, virtually all (95 percent) of married men with children in the household were employed. Two-thirds (65 percent) of wives in such families were employed. Husbands are still breadwinners, but so are wives. While employment does not typically eliminate a wife's dependency on her husband, it does mean that husbands are also dependent on wives. Most American marriages now involve a pooling of incomes. The resulting lifestyle, therefore, is produced jointly by wives and husbands. Income pooling has increasingly replaced the breadwinner/homemaker pattern.

Wasserman. © 1998 by *Boston Globe*. Distributed by Los Angeles Times Syndicate. Reprinted with permission.

These new economic realities of married life have not been fully incorporated into the institution of normative marriage—the way we think about marriage. Husbands and wives have yet to reconcile their joint economic dependency with the routine of married life. Even if most married couples today depend on one another's earnings, traditional patterns of domestic responsibilities persist. Such gendered marriages are a problem because they do not fit with the assumptions about men and women in all other spheres of their lives. . . .

What is the problem with marriage? The problem is the role of gender in the institution. More accurately, the problem is how to deal with widespread social change in matters of gender. But there is good reason to believe that we will come to terms with such challenges. Few boys today will grow up with mothers who are not employed. Young men are unlikely to inherit their fathers' or grandfathers' traditional views about marriage or women. Fewer men work with colleagues who openly view women and wives in traditional restricted roles. More and more of the youthful life course is spent in nontraditional families or outside of families altogether. Children, especially boys, who experience such childhoods (employed mothers, divorce, non-family living) are more accepting of women's new roles and options and are willing to perform more housework. It is not, therefore, a dramatic change in the basic institution of normative marriage that we need. Rather, it is a recognition and accommodation to the changes in women's lives and patience for intergenerational (cohort) change to catch up with current expectations. And men must become a part of the gender revolution. Even if this is not a fundamental redefinition of marriage, it will have profound consequences for how marriage is experienced because the tension between public and private lives will be reduced. . . .

Spousal Dependency

Proposals that marriage be recognized, promoted, and protected by revisions in federal tax codes, increased use of premarital counseling, and revisions in divorce laws are a good start. I believe we must go further, however, to create and reinforce dependencies in marriage. Dependency based automatically on gender will eventually be purged from marriage, as it is now being purged from work, school, and other public realms. The transition is clearly difficult and painful as we now can see. But what will bind couples to such new families? The answer is that bases of dependency other than gender must be created. Significant benefits must flow from the marriage, and significant exit costs must exist for both partners.

The most sensible, though controversial way to achieve these goals is for states to establish a preference for married couples in the distribution of discretionary benefits. My research on covenant marriage [in which couples must undergo premarital counseling and traditional fault-grounds for divorce] has convinced me that any attempt to privilege marriage over other statuses will be controversial and resisted, especially by those who see traditional marriage as unfair to women. Since the inequities in marriage are being resolved, I would focus on ways to privilege marriage by granting significant economic benefits to couples willing to commit to a restrictive regime. The purpose would be to create a new distinction between married and unmarried persons, though not one automatically based on gender. If marriage is to thrive, significant benefits other than emotional ones must flow from the status. And men and women alike must benefit from the status of marriage.

Marriage has traditionally been founded on dependencies of many types. But unequal (i.e. women's) economic dependencies are the most obvious (and often the source of inequity). In a world where men and women may each be economically independent, the benefits of pooled incomes may not suffice to sustain couples during those inevitable times when love fades. What Jean Bethke Elshtain, in her article "A Call to Civil Society," refers to as "the philosophy of expressive individualism"—a belief in the "sovereignty of the self" is fostered by gender equality and individual economic independence. In the absence of unequal economic dependencies, marriage must become a privileged status again, or else divorce rates will remain high, and marriage rates will continue to fall. To make it a privileged status, we should establish significant economic incentives. To the extent that people benefit economically in obvious and large ways by virtue of their marriages, (and to the extent that such benefits are not available to unmarried people) each spouse is dependent on the union, per se (dependency is typically measured by the costs of exiting a relationship).

Public Policy

The state has an enormous economic interest in promoting stable marriages. Strangely, the macroeconomic costs of divorce are rarely discussed in deliberations about public policy. Yet the microeconomic consequences are well known. Divorce and single-parenthood take a toll on earnings, educational attainment, labor-force attachment, subsequent marital stability, and the likelihood of poverty for the adults and the children involved. The aggregate consequences of all such individual losses are vast, even if unknown. Promoting marriage makes very good economic sense, beyond any other benefits to children or adults.

There are many ways we might promote marriage. Here I offer one example. We should consider significant tax credits for some married couples to create an economic interest in the marital union and significant exit costs for both partners. Americans will not tolerate mandatory family policy, so states should follow the lead of Louisiana in offering couples the option of two marriage regimes. Any couple could elect to be married under the customary no-fault divorce system without requirements for pre-marital and marital counseling. . . .

Couples who marry under the more restrictive marriage regime would qualify for very significant tax credits. Such credits must be quite large—$2,500 or $3,500 a year—sufficient to offset the costs of a college education for the children of married parents, or to underwrite the costs of a home, for example. Such tax credits would create a financial interest in the marriage per se, a benefit that flows to married couples by virtue of their marital status and nothing else. It also creates a significant exit cost at divorce. Both partners benefit so long as they remain married, both lose at divorce. How will we pay for such generous benefits? In fact, it is not certain that there would be net costs. A more appropriate question is how we will continue to pay for single parenthood and divorce.

Periodical Bibliography

The following articles have been selected to supplement the diverse views presented in this chapter.

David Blankenhorn   "A City with Foundations," *American Values*, October 10, 2001.

Stephanie Coontz   "Nostalgia as Ideology," *American Prospect*, April 8, 2002.

Jean Bethke Elshtain   "Philosophic Reflections on the Family at Millennium's Beginning," *World & I*, March 2000.

Maggie Gallagher   "Why Marriage Is Good for You," *City Journal*, Autumn 2000.

Robert P. George   "The 28th Amendment: It Is Time to Protect Marriage, and Democracy, in America," *National Review*, July 23, 2001.

Janet C. Gornick   "Reconcilable Differences: What It Would Take for Marriage and Feminism to Say I Do," *American Prospect*, April 8, 2002.

Stanley N. Kurtz   "What Is Wrong with Gay Marriage," *Commentary*, September 2000.

Francine Russo   "Bridal Vows Revisited," *Time*, July 24, 2000.

Jane Smiley   "Why Marriage?" *Harper's Magazine*, June 2000.

Judith Stacey and Timothy J. Biblarz   "(How) Does the Sexual Orientation of Parents Matter?" *American Sociologist Review*, April 2001.

Richard Weissbourd   "How Society Keeps Fathers Away from Their Children," *American Prospect*, December 6, 1999.

Barbara Dafoe Whitehead and David Popenoe   "Defining Daddy Down," *American Enterprise*, September 1999.

James Q. Wilson   "Why We Don't Marry," *City Journal*, Winter 2002.

Karl Zinsmeister   "Fatherhood Is Not for Wimps," *American Enterprise*, September 1999.

CHAPTER 3

Does Adoption Benefit Families?

Chapter Preface

In 1997, then-president Bill Clinton signed the Adoption and Safe Families Act (ASFA) into law. This law marks a shift away from the theory of "family preservation"—the belief that efforts should be made to reunite abused or neglected children with their biological parents—and toward "permanency planning." The goal of permanency planning is to find permanent adoptive homes for abused and neglected children as soon as possible.

Prior to the enactment of the ASFA, the Adoption Assistance and Child Welfare Act of 1980 guided American adoption policies. This act emphasized family preservation and regarded adoption as an action that took place only after reasonable efforts to reunify a family had failed. The term "reasonable efforts" has come to describe programs designed to help disadvantaged or troubled parents take care of their children. These include education, job training, substance abuse programs, and counseling. Other efforts that promote family preservation include kinship care arrangements, in which a child's relatives are encouraged to become his or her legal guardians.

Creators of the ASFA claimed that increasing numbers of children entering foster care highlighted the pressing need to place more of them into adoption. Moreover, ASFA advocates maintained that measures to reunite children with their biological parents had not only increased the number of children entering foster care but lengthened their stays in the foster care system. Critics of family preservation argue that this trend is problematic because children in the foster care system are at greater risk for abuse than children who are adopted or live with their biological families. According to journalist Melissa August, "Often [children in foster care] are held hostage to abuse and neglect, to bureaucratic foul-ups and carelessness, condemned to futures in which dreams cannot come true."

The ASFA has had some success in helping to remove children from foster care and placing them with adoptive families. In 1996, approximately 28,000 children in the United States were adopted out of foster care. In 1998, after the ASFA was passed, the number rose to 36,000. The following year, 46,000 children were adopted, surpassing that year's goal of 41,000. So far, the Department of Health and Human Services has awarded financial bonuses to forty-two states for increasing their adoption of foster care children. These figures reflect society's shift from efforts to preserve biological ties to finding loving, permanent adoptive homes for needy children.

Adoption is one of the most controversial issues facing American families today. Whether adoption is the best solution for removing children from foster care is one of the issues debated in the following chapter.

"Children adopted early in infancy do essentially as well . . . as children in the general population."

Adoption Should Be Encouraged

Elizabeth Bartholet

According to Elizabeth Bartholet, children who are adopted early in infancy fare as well as children who are raised by their biological parents. In addition, she argues that adoption is the best option for troubled children who cannot return to their homes because of abuse or neglect. Putting such children up for adoption is far preferable to returning them to their biological parents or the foster care system, Bartholet contends. Bartholet is a law professor and the author of *Nobody's Children: Abuse, Neglect, Foster Drift, and the Adoption Alternative*, from which the following excerpt was taken.

As you read, consider the following questions:
1. What are three recently enacted initiatives designed to increase the number of adopted children, as cited by Bartholet?
2. What evidence does the author cite to support her view that people are willing to adopt children with special needs?
3. According to Bartholet, why does the public stigmatize adoption?

Elizabeth Bartholet, *Nobody's Children: Abuse, Neglect, Foster Drift, and the Adoption Alternative*. Boston, MA: Beacon Press, 2000, pp. 18–24. Copyright © 2000 by Beacon Press. Reproduced with permission.

There is a lot of positive talk about adoption today, and some action. One can easily get the sense that a revolution is in the works. [Former president Bill Clinton] has announced his Adoption 2002 initiative, calling for a doubling in the number of children adopted out of foster care. Congress has passed within the space of just a few years several pieces of legislation designed to promote adoption. New federal laws ban racial barriers to adoption, limit the excesses of family-preservation policies, encourage child welfare agencies to move more children at earlier stages into adoptive homes, and encourage potential adoptive parents by giving them tax credits for adoption expenses. State and local leaders have initiated reforms to place renewed emphasis on children's safety and welfare, and to make adoption a higher policy priority. And in the last few years the number of adoptions has been rising, with some states showing dramatic increases.

Today's talk of adoption, and some new initiatives in the works, raise the hope that our society might be ready to make genuine changes in its child welfare system, taking adoption seriously for the first time as an option for children whose parents are not capable of parenting. But it will take a lot of work to turn that hope into reality.

The Need for Adoption

Estimates indicate that as of 1998 roughly 110,000 children in foster care had been freed for adoption, or had an adoption plan—about 20 percent of those in out-of-home care. Fifty-nine percent of these children are African-American, 29 percent are white, 10 percent are Hispanic, and 2 percent are of other races or ethnicities. But the need for adoption cannot be measured by these numbers. Many children are being kept in their families and in foster care, and shuffled back and forth between the two, for whom adoption should be considered, but is not. The claim has been that adoption wouldn't be good for them—that children are almost always best off with their parents. The assumption has been that adoption wouldn't be possible anyway—that the homes just aren't there for the black children, the damaged children, and the older children that dominate the foster care population.

The evidence is clear that adoption works, and that it is

the best of the available alternatives for children who have been subjected to abuse or neglect. This is true in terms of all the measures social scientists use to assess well-being, including measures of self-esteem and outcome measures related to later education, employment, crime and the like. It is also true in terms of abuse and neglect rates. Indeed, adopted children are less likely to suffer child abuse than is the norm in the general population of children raised by their biological parents.

Family preservationists' claim that adoption harms children by depriving them of their family and roots relies on speculative theories that adoptees suffer from "genealogical bewilderment" and the like. But empirical studies that assess how carefully selected samples and control groups of children actually fare in life, based on all the measures of human well-being that social scientists have devised, reveal no damage suffered by virtue of transferring children from their biological parents to adoptive parents. Children adopted early in infancy do essentially as well, on measures of self-esteem, attachment, and performance, as children in the general population. These studies confirm that what is central to children's welfare is that they be placed in an appropriately nurturing permanent home as early in life as possible.

1. But can adoption work for today's foster care population?

Adoption skeptics say no. They say that the children in foster care are too damaged, and many of them too old, for adoption to work. They point to the numbers who are born impaired by drugs and alcohol, the numbers who suffer from physical and mental disabilities, the numbers who have been subjected to extreme forms of abuse and neglect, and the numbers who are in their teens, having first suffered harm in their original homes, followed by many years adrift in the foster care system, or moving back and forth from foster homes to their homes of origin. They argue that while adoption might work for healthy infants, it can't work for these children. They note that significant numbers of adoptions from foster care "disrupt," with the children sent back from their adoptive homes into the foster care system. They claim that the only solutions for this damaged, older population of children lie in renewed emphasis on family preservation, on long-term foster care or guardianship, and on group or institutional homes.

But the evidence indicates that adoption can and does work for children who are damaged and for children who are older. These children do have extra-ordinary needs. Most of them are far more likely to find the extra-ordinary parenting they require to overcome their history and heal their injuries in the adoptive parent population than in the families that subjected them to abuse and neglect, or in temporary foster care, or in institutional care.

Children with Special Needs

A significant percentage of today's foster care and group home population are infants, many of whom were born showing the effects of their mother's use of alcohol and drugs during pregnancy. Many were removed as a result of their parents' substance abuse and related maltreatment during the period soon after birth. Drug experts have been arguing for years that "crack babies" and other infants whose mothers used licit and illicit drugs during pregnancy have a variety of special needs requiring special care, but that with that care they can flourish. These experts have advocated vigorously against simply writing off this generation of children and have testified specifically to their adoptability.

Studies of children who have suffered enormous emotional damage as a result of abuse and neglect, or wartime atrocities, show that adoption has the capacity to help many such children heal and recover, so that they can lead essentially normal lives. Adoption critics point to the adoption disruption statistics, but given the damage that so many foster care children have suffered, the fact that only roughly 10 percent of the adoptions out of the foster care system disrupt should be seen as a mark of the success achieved in these adoptive relationships. Studies of special-needs adoptions generally show that these adoptive families form the same kind of loving, committed, and satisfying family relationships as those formed in other adoptive families.

It is true that some older children in foster care have developed meaningful ties with biological parents, but adoption need not destroy such ties. There is an increasing tendency toward openness in adoption which would allow children to gain the permanence and committed parenting of an adoptive family, while maintaining healthy links with their family of origin.

Adoption Creates Families

Adoption is not a problem. Adoption is a solution. There are people all over this country who would like to be parents, and who would be fine parents, but who are not able to grow babies. There are children all over this world who no longer have parents, or whose parents are unable to care for them. When these two get together, it is not a trauma. It is not a minefield. There's a word for it. It's called a family.

Marjorie Hershey, *Adoptive Families*, March/April 1998.

It is also true that adoption works better for children when they are placed in infancy and when they have not been horribly damaged by abuse and neglect, or by the inconsistency and uncertainty in parenting arrangements characteristic of foster care. Adoption studies regularly confirm that age at the time of placement is the key predictor for how well adopted children will do. This is no surprise. And it is obviously no argument for giving up on adoption as a solution for the foster care population. Adoption will still work better for most foster children than any other option, although it is undoubtedly true that some children are so damaged by the maltreatment they suffered or by their experience in the child welfare system that they have to be relegated to institutional care.

Helping Children Early

These adoption studies *are* an argument for moving children out of their biological homes and on to adoptive homes as soon as it is reasonably clear that they are not likely to receive the kind of care from their parents that they need to thrive. Delay in adoption may not necessarily permanently destroy children. But abuse and neglect combined with foster drift injure children in ways that not only cause suffering but also damage their life prospects, diminishing the chances for them to flourish in the way that children adopted as infants typically do flourish. All too many foster children today *are* older and *have* suffered damage, and *do* as a result have diminished life prospects even in adoption. But these are realities that are in our power to change.

2. But can adoptive families be found for today's foster care population?

Adoption skeptics say no. They argue that potential adoptive parents are limited in number and interested only in healthy infants, and that the whites who make up most of the adoptive parent pool are not interested in the nonwhite children who make up most of the foster care pool.

The reality is that we have done more to drive prospective parents away from the foster care system than to draw them in. We could expand the existing parent pool by recruiting broadly; now we recruit on the most limited basis. We could socialize prospective parents in ways that would open their minds to the idea of parenting children born to other parents and other racial groups, and children who have physical and mental disabilities; for the most part we now do just the opposite.

Increasing Demand

Skeptics talk as if the number of adoptive parents and the nature of their interests were fixed in stone. In fact the "demand" for adoption is extremely malleable. What exists today is a reality that our social policies have created. History demonstrates our power to reshape this reality. Prior to the mid-nineteenth century there was no apparent interest in adoption, because there was no legal mechanism enabling adoption. It took legislative and administrative action setting up an adoption system before adoptive parents could step forward, but now that such a system has been created we have well over 100,000 adoptions per year, more than half of which are adoptions by nonrelatives. Prior to World War II there was no apparent interest in international adoption, but now that systems have been set up enabling prospective parents to adopt children from abroad, many thousands of foreign children per year come into the United States to be adopted by U.S. citizens—15,774 in fiscal year 1998. Until a couple of decades ago, the only children considered adoptable were healthy infants. Now that efforts have been made to recruit parents for children with disabilities, there are waiting lists for Down's Syndrome children and for other children who used to be relegated to institutional care. Even children with extreme disabilities have been placed by child welfare agencies that have made the effort to reach out to locate and educate potential adopters. NACAC—the North American Council on Adoptable Children—says that *no child* in the foster care system should be considered unadoptable.

The potential pool of adoptive parents is enormous—it dwarfs the pool of waiting children. About 1.2 million women are infertile and 7.1 percent of married couples, or 2.1 million. The infertile are potentially a significant resource for children in need of homes, but at present only a limited number of them adopt. It is even more rare for the fertile to think of adoption as a way to build, or add to, their family. About 1 percent of women age 18–44, or 500,000, are currently seeking to adopt. Only 0.2 percent, or 100,000, had applied to an adoption agency. It is safe to assume that millions more would have pursued adoption had our social policies encouraged rather than discouraged them.

Ours is a society that glorifies reproduction, drives the infertile to pursue treatment at all costs, socializes them to think of adoption as a second-class form of parenting to be pursued only as a last resort, and regulates adoption in a way that makes it difficult, degrading, and expensive. We could instead encourage not only the infertile but the fertile to think of adoption as a normal way to build their families. We now ask young couples when they are going to have their first baby. We could ask them when they are thinking of expanding their family, and whether they are thinking about adoption or procreation or both. We could encourage all adult members of our society to think that their responsibility as members of the national community includes caring for the youngest members of that community when care is needed. . . .

Providing a Future

We know better than we do. We know that children require nurturing environments to thrive today and to have promising prospects for tomorrow. Common sense, confirmed by the research, tells us that children who are severely abused and neglected will do best if removed and placed permanently with families where they will receive the kind of nurturing likely to help them recover from their wounds. Common sense, confirmed by the research, tells us they would do better yet if we moved them when abuse and neglect were first manifest. This does not mean that in all cases of severe abuse and neglect we should immediately terminate the parents' rights and move children on to adoption. But it does mean that we should consider immediate termination of parental rights in many more cases and place a much higher priority on prompt adoptive placement.

We also know, or should know, that once we decide that children cannot be adequately nurtured in their homes of origin, they will be best off if we focus not simply on keeping them connected with their roots, but on taking care of them today in a way that will enable them to function tomorrow. Richard Barth, of the Jordan Institute for Families at the University of North Carolina School of Social Work, stands out as one of the few scholars willing to state the obvious: that for children to thrive it is important that we focus not just on their past but on their present and their future; that it matters if they are brought up by people who are capable of nurturing them, and in schools and communities where they can learn and be safe from violence.

"Adoption is ethically wrong and morally indefensible."

Adoption Should Be Abolished

Evelyn Burns Robinson

In the following viewpoint, Evelyn Burns Robinson argues that adoption is wrong because it is a permanent solution to temporary problems. She contends that instead of promoting adoption, society should help mothers struggling with poverty or mental illness. Robinson believes that the biological ties between mother and child should never be severed. Robinson is a former high school teacher and a social worker with the Association Representing Mothers Separated from their Children (ARMS). She is the author of *Adoption and Loss: The Hidden Grief*, the source of the following viewpoint.

As you read, consider the following questions:

1. What "humane alternative" to adoption was enacted by the New Zealand government in 2000, according to Robinson?
2. What solution does the author propose for assisting children who are not safe with their natural parents?
3. According to Robinson, what is the only appropriate situation for separating a child from his or her parents?

There is no justification for adoption. Why do some governments persist in issuing adopted children with new birth certificates, which are a fabrication? It is offensive to natural mothers to find that both their existence and their experience are so easily obliterated with the stroke of a pen. Adopted people also object to their original details being officially erased. [Therapist Betty Jean] Lifton describes how, because of the fact that they are issued with a new birth certificate, adopted people grow up believing that their 'birth heritage is disposable.' [Feminist Joss] Shawyer describes the falsification of birth records as, 'an insult to personal dignity.'

Changing Practices

Our moral awareness is continually growing. Policies and practices that once were acceptable are no longer tolerated. Slavery was legal in the United States until just over a hundred years ago. Now it is abhorred. In 1999, we are appalled to think that communities once bought and sold people, uprooting them from their families and transplanting them elsewhere. To us, it is clear that slavery is ethically wrong and morally indefensible. We wonder how apparently upright, moral people, such as ministers of religion, could not only defend but practise slavery, extolling its virtues. Slavery's defenders pointed out that slaves were better off being owned by a good master, that it provided them with a home and security and rescued them from a life of disadvantage. Slaves were expected to be grateful. It took a long time for these ideas to be challenged. Now we take for granted the basic human right of freedom, the respect for human dignity that does not allow trade in human beings. Why did people buy slaves? Because they wanted them and society said that they could.

In some countries, such as Australia, adoption is still legal. In some countries it has never existed and never will. In such places, people would react with horror to the very idea of permanently changing the parenthood and genealogy of a child. Adoption's defenders describe how adoption saves children from a lifetime of disadvantage, gives them security and a good home, for which they should be grateful. Does that sound familiar? Why did people adopt children? Because they wanted them and society said that they could.

It is time for society to realise that adoption is ethically wrong and morally indefensible. The idea that adoption is socially acceptable needs to be strenuously challenged. People need to be educated to see adoption for what it is, and to abandon it, in the same way that they had to be educated to denounce slavery.

Sadly, most academics who write about adoption take it as a given and do not question its existence. [Professor David] Howe et al, for example, write about, '. . . the conditions that make adoption necessary.' There are no conditions that make adoption necessary, because *adoption is not necessary* and it never has been necessary. Adoption was a social experiment. The tragic outcomes of this experiment make it clear that the way ahead must be a future without adoption. Robert Ludbrook, a lawyer and founding member of Jigsaw, presented an interesting paper at the Adoption and Healing Conference in New Zealand in 1997 entitled *Closing the Wound*, subtitled, *An Argument for the Abolition of Adoption*. In it he explains why he believes that, '. . . adoption no longer serves any overriding social purpose which outweighs its negative aspects.' At the time of writing this [viewpoint], January 2000, the New Zealand government is considering the question of whether or not to abolish adoption and replace it with a system of "legal parenthood" which would convey the rights and responsibilities of parenthood without changing the child's identity and without involving secrecy and inaccessible records. It will be very interesting to see if New Zealand has the courage to take the lead in putting an end to adoption and putting the effort into creating a more humane alternative. ["Legal parenthood" was enacted that same year.]

Suffer the Children and Mothers

Mothers grieve for the loss of their children and children grieve for the loss of their mothers. Natural mothers and adopted people deserve appropriate services to assist them to deal with their grief, but we must be very careful to distinguish between addressing the needs of those whose lives have already been affected by adoption and preventing further grief. There is no evidence, to my knowledge, that providing counselling before removing women's children from them will prevent them suffering from future grief reactions associated with the loss of those children. There is no "right" way to perform a permanent, legal separation of a mother from her child. Regardless of any counselling which occurs, these mothers will still have to deal with the fact that they have apparently voluntarily given away their children and that their children still exist and so their loss will never be final. Those mothers whose children are taken from them without their consent are still considered to be responsible, as the separation has apparently been caused by their failure to provide a safe home environment for their children. Neither is any amount of counselling for mothers at the time of separating them from their children going to help those children to come to terms with their loss. Mothers and children separated by adoption grieve because they have been separated. Extenuating factors exacerbate their grief, but the actual cause of the grief is the separation itself.

Adoption Commodifies Children

The child is never a party to the "contract" which transforms him into an adoptee. Both adoptees and parents are subjected to inhuman and degrading treatment when there is needless separation of the child from the parent, when the system and special interests commodify the child according to "supply and demand," and when adoption is pursued as a punitive response to illegitimacy, unwed parenthood, poverty or social class. Closed adoption in particular is regarded by activists as a form of child abuse.

Lori Carangelo, www.abolishadoption.com, updated July 4, 2002.

There are certainly children, sadly, who are not safe with their natural families. How are we to care for them? A safe environment needs to be found for them, preferably with members of their extended family or social circle, in a situation with which they are already familiar. Family links should be maintained at all costs. There is never any need for a permanent, legal separation of parents and children. If there are children who are genuinely not safe growing up with their original families and find themselves growing up with those to whom they are not related, their original names and identities must be maintained. There must be no more pretence and denial. These children have a right to know who they are and to whom they are related.

Adoption has traditonally been used as a punishment for the parents, although welfare agencies would not admit to this. What they fail to realise is that this separation is also a punishment for the children. Separating parents from children does not teach the parents to modify their behaviour, nor does it offer them any hope or incentive to do so. It does not teach them parenting skills; it also does not prevent the parents from having more children. If our current foster care system is not serving children well, that is no excuse to continue to have them adopted. That is a reason to improve the service we can provide to children in need. The whole system of alternative care for children needs to be redesigned with the best interests of children in mind. We need to look closely at foster care and at guardianship so that we can provide what children need, whether it is short term or long term care. Our children deserve the best care that we can provide for them. I have great admiration for those who open their homes to children in need, expecting nothing in return but the satisfaction of knowing that they have made a difference. There is a trend in many countries now towards family preservation programmes, in which efforts are made to keep families together. Hopefully, these will gradually take the place of adoption policies, which actually cause family breakdown.

Feeling Secure

There are some who say that children need the security of adoption. Children do, certainly, benefit from a feeling of security, but they do not necessarily obtain that from being adopted. In fact, it is not an adoption order that provides children with security. In many cases people adopt a child only to decide after some time that they no longer want the child. The child is then returned to the authorities, sometimes fostered, sometimes re-adopted. It is unconditional love that provides children with a feeling of security, not a piece of paper. Many children feel happy and secure living with people who are not their parents, regardless of whether they are adopted or not and, sadly, many children do not feel appreciated, nor secure, living with their natural or adoptive parents. Adoptive parents sometimes divorce and separate, they abuse and neglect their children, just as natural parents do. What children in need of care certainly do deserve is to maintain their identity and their links with their families and to grow up with honesty and openness. Our children and our families deserve the best possible service in times of crisis.

There seems to be a growing emphasis, especially in the United States, on the provision of material possessions. Young women are still being pressured into giving away their children simply because they are in a disadvantaged position (which is probably temporary) financially. This emphasis is quite inappropriate and very saddening. A sense of belonging and of being valued cannot be bought. I am sure that if a random sample of the adult population was questioned about their fondest childhood memories, very few of them would mention the amount of money that was spent on them. Children and their parents should only be separated when there is an issue of the child's safety, not ever simply because someone else is in a position to spend more money on that child.

Women must stop taking other women's children. If a woman is unable to care for her child because she lacks the skills, then we should try to teach her the skills. If a woman is temporarily in a situation that would be unsafe for her child, then by all means care for the child elsewhere, but in the meantime help the woman to get out of her dangerous situation. If poverty is the issue, then strategies need to be put in place to address the poverty. Women in trouble need support. They do not need to be made to feel even more powerless by being robbed of their children. We must stop using the *permanent* practice of adoption to solve what are often *temporary* problems. If there is a permanently unsuitable situation, for example where the mother suffers from a mental health problem which would put her child at risk, then we should arrange for the child to be cared for elsewhere, but should not abandon and punish the mother. Both mother and child will benefit from enjoying an on-going, if necessary supervised, relationship. There is no justification in such cases for changing the child's identity and pretending that the child has a different mother. If a woman wishes to have a child and is unable to, she has no right to take a child from another woman to fulfil her desire. Adoption is largely a women's issue as women are the ones who bear children. Men, unfortunately, are most often the ones who make adoption policies. Women must make their voices heard and force changes to outdated adoption policies. . . .

Adoption Touches Numerous Lives

For each adoption that takes place, many people are affected. Each adopted person has four parents, they may have siblings in their adoptive family and siblings in their natural family (say two of each), they may have a partner themselves and children of their own, perhaps two. This makes an average of twelve people directly affected by each adoption, before we even consider grandparents and other extended family members. In the United States it has been estimated that there are currently six million adopted people. World-wide, there is a vast number of people whose lives have been directly affected by adoption. These are the casualties of adoption. At the International Conference on Adoption and Healing held in New Zealand in 1997, Keith Griffith said, 'Healing needs to be more than running an ambulance at the bottom of the cliff. It must also demand the removal of factors that push people over the top.'

Perhaps now we can all recognise that those whose lives have been affected by adoption have been damaged by the experience and are entitled to assistance and support. It is time for society to acknowledge that the grief of those who have been separated by adoption is legitimate and is, in fact, the appropriate, expected response to their experiences. Hopefully the community in general will now realise that family members who have been separated by adoption are still family members and that it is natural and commendable for them to wish to know each other. Let us hope that we can look forward to a more enlightened future, where parents are supported to raise their own children and where everyone recognises that it is wrong to take another person's child, no matter what the circumstances.

> *"Children who grow up with . . . gay or lesbian parents fare as well . . . as do children whose parents are heterosexual."*

Gays and Lesbians Should Have the Right to Adopt

Albert R. Hunt

In the following viewpoint, Albert R. Hunt argues that prohibiting adoptions by gay and lesbian couples hurts children. Hunt contends that denying homosexual couples the right to adopt relegates more children to foster care than is necessary. In addition, he maintains that children raised by gay parents do as well as children reared by heterosexual parents. Hunt is an executive editor at the *Wall Street Journal*.

As you read, consider the following questions:

1. According to the author, how has Bill Clinton improved adoption policies for gay and lesbian couples?
2. What arguments do the "homophobic right" use to support their rejection of homosexual adoptions, as stated by the author?
3. According to Hunt, how are homosexual adoptions similar to transracial adoptions?

Imagine breaking up families and sentencing thousands of kids to perpetual foster care. Yet, under the guise of family values, that's exactly what some social conservatives would do.

Groups like the Family Research Council, and the Traditional Values Coalition, headed by renowned hate monger Lou Sheldon, want to deny gays and lesbians the right to adopt children. Unfortunately this put-these-kids-last posture has the backing of both President George W. Bush and his brother, Florida Governor Jeb Bush.

Getting Real

In a perfect world, each of the more than 100,000 kids waiting to be adopted would be taken in by a caring, responsible husband and wife. But, as Adam Pertman, author of *Adoption Nation: How the Adoption Revolution is Transforming America*, notes: "It's far from a perfect world when it comes to adoption." Most kids who can't fit into that perfect world are better off with single parents or gay and lesbian parents.

The issue crystallized when a federal judge upheld a mean-spirited quarter-century-old Florida law that bans adoption by gays or lesbians. There are only two other states, Mississippi and Utah, that prohibit adoptions by gay couples, but there are efforts to make it more difficult elsewhere.

This is hypocrisy writ large. Gay and lesbian couples in Florida can adopt a child in most other states, so it's the kids who are hurt. Moreover, while the social right insists on the sanctity of married couple adoptions, one out of four Florida adoptions is by a single parent.

With the work of former president Bill Clinton, America's most pro-adoption president, and sympathetic GOP congressional leaders, adoption is on the upswing. There are more generous tax breaks, states are rewarded for moving kids more expeditiously out of foster care, and transracial barriers are eroding. In 2000, the number of kids adopted from the public foster-care system doubled from five years earlier to 50,000.

Still, the supply outstrips the demand. There were 134,000 children waiting to be adopted in 2000. These aren't babies. On average they are over eight years of age and have been waiting for more than three years.

Support from the Experts

The American Academy of Pediatricians recently supported gay adoptions or, more precisely, second-parent adoptions in same-sex couples: "Children who grow up with one or two gay or lesbian parents fare as well in emotional, cognitive, social and sexual functioning as do children whose parents are heterosexual," the pediatricians reported.

"We looked at a lot of data and there is no support for a commonly held belief that these kids are at special risk or do poorly," says Dr. Joseph Hagan, a Burlington, V.T., pediatrician who chaired the committee that directed the study.

Other medical associations and prominent adoption advocates, such as the Dave Thomas Center for Adoption, support this view. But the homophobic right went ballistic. Lou Sheldon labeled the pediatricians a "homosexual" group that wanted to tear down the American family. The Family Research Council insisted data showed this is "incontrovertibly inconsistent" with raising healthy kids. Foes of gay and lesbian adoptions, frequently cite a study by two University of Southern California academics published in the *American Sociological Review*, which they claim proves harmful effects of gay and lesbian parenting.

"That is totally false," replies sociologist Judith Stacey, one of the authors of that study. "They use phony research and then egregiously distort real research."

Professor Stacey's study, actually a review of all the surveys on the subject, paralleled the pediatricians' conclusions. There was one very small British study involving about 50 children which showed kids with a gay or lesbian parent are more inclined to have a homosexual experience. But, she says, that's not conclusive.

Caring for Kids with Special Needs

It also is largely irrelevant to current realities. Hard data on adoption is remarkably elusive—the census asked an adoption question for the first time in 2000—but the very reliable Evan B. Donaldson Institute estimates that 30% to 40% of kids in foster care are physically disabled, and as many as 60% have some sort of psychological disorder. There's considerable anecdotal evidence suggesting gays and lesbians dis-

Research on Lesbian and Gay Parenting

All of the research to date has reached the same unequivocal conclusion about gay parenting: the children of lesbian and gay parents grow up as successfully as the children of heterosexual parents. In fact, not a single study has found the children of lesbian or gay parents to be disadvantaged because of their parents' sexual orientation. Other key findings include:

- There is no evidence to suggest that lesbians and gay men are unfit to be parents.

- Home environments with lesbian and gay parents are as likely to successfully support a child's development as those with heterosexual parents.

- Good parenting is not influenced by sexual orientation. Rather, it is influenced most profoundly by a parent's ability to create a loving and nurturing home—an ability that does not depend on whether a parent is gay or straight.

- There is no evidence to suggest that the children of lesbian and gay parents are less intelligent, suffer from more problems, are less popular, or have lower self-esteem than children of heterosexual parents.

- The children of lesbian and gay parents grow up as happy, healthy and well-adjusted as the children of heterosexual parents.

American Civil Liberties Union, Fact Sheet: Overview of Lesbian and Gay Parenting, Adoption and Foster Care, April 6, 1999.

---

proportionately are willing to take these hard-to-adopt kids.

In the Florida case, two gay men wanted to adopt a 10-year-old, HIV-positive boy they'd cared for since he was an infant. Governor Bush's administration also is fighting the efforts of another gay man to adopt a 9-year-old boy he's cared for ever since he was abandoned by his parents.

There are an estimated 3,400 foster care kids in Florida waiting for adoption. Many, like these two children, suffer special disadvantages. If gays or lesbians aren't permitted to adopt these kids, there is only one recourse: they'll stay in foster care. So when Ken Conner, the president of the Family Research Council, says there's no justification for adoption by a gay or lesbian couple, he sends a simple message to these children: Let them rot.

"We're not talking about kids where there's a long line

around the block to adopt," notes Mr. Pertman. "Many of these are the hardest kids to get anybody to take. How anyone justifies putting a child in the ninth foster home in seven years rather than be adopted by someone who wants them is beyond me."

The situation is analogous to the fight over transracial adoption. African-American social workers long argued that to allow whites to adopt black children amounted to "racial genocide." Since there weren't enough prospective African-American adoptive parents, this meant relegating these minority kids to perpetual foster care.

But Bill Clinton backed an effort spearheaded by liberal Democratic Senator Howard Metzenbaum to break down this barrier. It's okay to give an African-American preference in adopting a baby of the same race. But if that's not possible, it's no longer permissible to block a transracial adoption. This is precisely what ought to be done with gay or lesbian adoptions in Florida and elsewhere.

Enhancing adoption in America is putting kids first. Bill Clinton was right to take on one of his constituencies, black social workers, to further this goal. It will be instructive to see whether Jeb and George W. Bush likewise care more about these kids who need homes, or are more interested in pandering to one of their constituencies, the homophobic right.

*"[Homosexual adoptions] would cause
problems for numerous children."*

Gays and Lesbians Should Not Have the Right to Adopt

Paul Cameron

In the following viewpoint, Paul Cameron argues that groups recommending that gays and lesbians be allowed to adopt misrepresent studies on the effects of gay and lesbian parenting. Cameron charges that such groups care more about identity politics than they do about children. The fact is, he maintains, numerous studies prove that the children of gay and lesbian couples have more emotional problems and perform worse at school than children of heterosexual parents. Cameron is chairman of the Family Research Council Institute in Colorado Springs, Colorado.

As you read, consider the following questions:
1. As stated by the author, what are the three sets of information on the issue of homosexual adoption?
2. According to Cameron, what was the difference in self-esteem between children of homosexual parents and those of heterosexual parents?
3. What is an example the author gives of how gay-rights activists manipulate data to serve their own ends?

Paul Cameron, "Symposium—Q: Does Adoption By Gay or Lesbian Couples Put American Children at Risk? Yes: The Conclusions of the American Academy of Pediatrics Are Not to Be Believed," *Insight on the News*, Vol. 18, April 22, 2002, pp. 40–44. Copyright © 2002 by News World Communications, Inc. Reproduced with permission.

On February 4, 2000, the American Academy of Pediatrics (AAP) recommended "legal and legislative efforts" to allow children "born to or adopted by one member of a gay or lesbian couple" to be adopted by the homosexual partner. Such a law effectively would eliminate the possibility of adoption by other family members following the death of the parent. It also would cause problems for numerous children.

The AAP, like many other professional organizations, apparently was too caught up in promoting identity politics to address all the evidence relevant to homosexual adoption. In its report, the organization offered only positive evidence about gays and lesbians as parents. "In fact," the report concluded, "growing up with parents who are lesbian or gay may confer some advantages to children." Really?

Problems with Homosexual Parents

There are three sets of information on the issue: clinical reports of psychiatric disturbance of children with homosexual parents, testimonies of children with homosexual parents concerning their situation and studies that have compared the children of homosexuals with the children of nonhomosexuals. The AAP ignored the first two sets and had to cherry-pick the comparative studies to arrive at the claim that "[n]o data have pointed to any risk to children as a result of growing up in a family with one or more gay parents."

A number of clinical reports detail "acting-out behavior," homosexual seduction, elective muteness and the desire for a mother by children with homosexual parents. I am unaware of a single child being disturbed because his mother and father were married.

The AAP also ignored the testimonies of children with homosexual parents—probably the best evidence since these kids had to "live with it" rather than deal with a theory. More than 150 children with homosexual parents have provided, in extensive interviews, detailed evidence of the difficulties they encountered as a result. A study Paul and Kirk Cameron published this year in Psychological Reports analyzed the content of 57 life-story narratives by children with homosexual parents assembled by lesbian researchers Louise Rafkin (United States) and Lisa Saffron (Britain).

In these narratives, children in 48 of the 52 families (92 percent) mentioned one or more "problems." Of the 213 problems which were scored—including hypersexuality, instability, molestation, domestic violence—children attributed 201 (94 percent) to their homosexual parent(s).

Here are four sample excerpts:

• One 9-year-old girl said: "My biological mother is S. and my other mother is L. We've lived together for a year. Before that L. lived across the street. . . . My mom met L.; L. had just broken up with someone. We moved in together because it got complicated going back and forth every night. All of a sudden I felt like I was a different person because my mom was a lesbian. . . . I get angry because I can't tell anybody about my mom. The kids at school would laugh. . . . They say awful things about lesbians . . . then they make fun of me. Having lesbian mothers is nothing to laugh about. . . . I have told my [mother] that she has made my life difficult."

• A 12-year-old boy in the United Kingdom said: "Mum . . . has had several girlfriends in my lifetime. . . . I don't go around saying that I've got two mums. . . . If we are sitting in a restaurant eating, she'll say, 'I want you to know about all these sex things.' And she'll go on about everything, just shouting it out. . . . Sometimes when mum embarrasses me, I think, 'I wish I had a dad.' . . . Been to every gay pride march. Last year, while attending, we went up to a field . . . when two men came up to us. One of them started touching me. I didn't want to go this year because of that."

• According to a 39-year-old woman: "In my memories, I'm always looking for my mother and finding her with a woman doing things I don't understand. . . . Sometimes they blame me for opening a door that wasn't even locked. . . . [At about the age of 10], I noticed a door that I hadn't yet opened. Inside I saw a big bed. My mother sat up suddenly and stared at me. She was with B. . . . and then B. shouted, 'You f***ing sneaking brat!' My mother never said a word. [Then came N.] I came to hate N. because of the way she and my mother fought every night. They screamed and bickered and whined and pouted over everything. N. closed my mother's hand in the car door. . . . She and N. hadn't made love in seven years."

• According to a 19-year-old man: "When I was about 7, my mother told me that this woman, D., was going to stay with us for a while—and she never left! I didn't think anything much about it until I was about 10. . . . It just became obvious because she and my mother were sleeping together. A few months after D. left, my mother started to see another woman, but that didn't last. Then she got involved with a different woman . . . ; she'd be violent toward my mother. . . . After that she started to go on marches and to women's groups. . . . There were some women in these groups who objected to men altogether, and I couldn't cope with that.". . .

Academic Performance

The AAP ignored every comparative study of children that showed those with homosexual parents experiencing more problems. These include the largest comparative study, reported in 1996 by Sotirios Sarantakos in the journal, *Children Australia*, of 58 elementary schoolchildren raised by coupled homosexual parents who were closely matched (by age, sex, grade in school, social class) with 58 children of cohabiting heterosexual parents and 58 raised by married parents. Teachers reported that the married couples' children scored best at math and language but somewhat lower in social studies, experienced the highest level of parental involvement at school as well as at home and had parents with the highest expectations for them. The children of homosexuals scored lowest in math and language and somewhat higher in social studies, were the least popular, experienced the lowest level of parental involvement at school and at home, had parents with the lowest expectations for them and least frequently expressed higher educational and career expectations.

Yet the AAP said that studies have "failed to document any differences between such groups on . . . academic success." The organization's report also ignored the only empirical study based upon a random sample that reported on 17 adults (out of a sample of 5,182) with homosexual parents.

Detailed by Cameron and Cameron in the journal *Adolescence* in 1996, the 17 were disproportionately apt to report sexual relations with their parents, more apt to report a less than exclusively heterosexual orientation, more frequently reported gender dissatisfaction and were more apt to report that their first sexual experience was homosexual.

Asay. © 1999 by Colorado Springs Gazette Telegraph. Reprinted by permission of Creators Syndicate, Inc.

The AAP report also seemingly ignored a 1998 *Psychological Reports* study by Cameron and Cameron that included the largest number of children with homosexual parents. That study compared 73 children of homosexuals with 105 children of heterosexuals. Of the 66 problems cited by panels of judges who extensively reviewed the living conditions and psychological reactions of children of homosexuals undergoing a divorce from heterosexuals, 64 (97 percent) were attributed to the homosexual parent.

Misrepresenting Data

Finally, while ignoring studies that contradicted its own conclusions, the AAP misrepresented numerous findings from the limited literature it cited. Thus, researcher Sharon Huggins compared 18 children of 16 volunteer/lesbian mothers with 18 children of 16 volunteer/heterosexual/divorced mothers on self-esteem. Huggins reported statistically nonsignificant differences between the 19 children of mothers who were not living with a lover versus the 17 children of mothers who were living with a lover; and, further, that [the four] "adolescent daughters with high self-esteem had been told of their mother's lesbianism at a mean age of 6.0 years. In contrast, [the five] adolescent daughters with low self-esteem had been told at a mean age of 9.6 years" and "three of four of the mothers with high self-esteem daughters were currently living with lesbian lovers, but only one of four of the lesbian mothers with low self-esteem daughters was currently living with a lesbian lover."

The AAP cited Huggins as proving that "children's self-esteem has been shown to be higher among adolescents whose mothers (of any sexual orientation) were in a new partnered relationship after divorce, compared with those whose mother remained single, and among those who found out at a younger age that their parent was homosexual, compared with those who found out when they were older," thus transforming statistical nonevents based on niggling numbers of volunteers into important differences—twice in one sentence!

Risk of Early Death

We have examined more than 10,000 obituaries of homosexuals: The median age of death for lesbians was in the 40s to 50s; for homosexuals it was in the 40s. Most Americans live into their 70s. Yet in the 1996 U.S. government sex survey the oldest lesbian was 49 years old and the oldest gay 54.

Children with homosexual parents are considerably more apt to lose a parent to death. Indeed, a homosexual couple in their 30s is roughly equivalent to a nonhomosexual couple in their late 40s or 50s. Adoption agencies will seldom permit a couple in their late 40s or 50s adopt a child because of the risk of parental death, and the consequent social and psychological difficulty for the child. The AAP did not address this fact—one with profound implications for any child legally related to a homosexual.

As usual, the media picked up on the AAP report as authoritative, assuming that it represented the consensus of a large and highly educated membership. Not so. As in other professional organizations, the vast majority of members pay their dues, read the journal and never engage in professional politics. As a consequence, a small but active minority of members gains control and uses the organization to promote its agenda. Too often, the result is ideological literature that misrepresents the true state of knowledge.

Gay-rights activists have been particularly adept at manipulating research and reports to their own ends. For years the media reported that all studies revealed that 10 percent of the population was homosexual. In fact, few if any studies ever came to that conclusion. For the next few years we will have to live with the repeated generalization that all studies prove homosexual parents are as good for children as heterosexual parents, and perhaps even better. What little literature exists on the subject proves no such thing. Indeed, translated into the language of accounting, the AAP report could be described as "cooking the books."

Periodical Bibliography

The following articles have been selected to supplement the diverse views presented in this chapter.

Dan Allen
"The Adoption Option: Rosie O'Donnell and Tens of Thousands of Other Gay People Have Chosen to Adopt Children—But How Many Roadblocks Stand in the Way of Others Who Want to Follow Their Lead?" *Advocate*, May 28, 2002.

Stephanie Brill
"Overseas Adoptions: The Secret Everyone Is Talking About," *Curve*, May 2001.

Ira Carnahan
"The Rise of 'Bastard Nation'," *Human Life Review*, Winter 2001.

Kim Clarke and Nancy Shute
"The Adoption Maze," *U.S. News & World Report*, March 12, 2001.

Gill Donovan
"Inadequate Adoption Laws Exploit Families," *National Catholic Reporter*, December 12, 2001.

Jean Bethke Elshtain
"The Chosen Family: Adoption, or the Triumph of Love Over Biology," *New Republic*, September 14, 1998.

Ivor Gaber
"A Child Needs a Parent of Any Race," *New Statesman*, September 4, 1998.

Ellen Herman
"Families Made By Science: Arnold Gesell and the Technologies of Modern Child Adoption," *Isis*, December 2001.

Leslie Doty Hollingsworth
"Promoting Same-Race Adoption for Children of Color," *Social Work*, March 1998.

Irving G. Leon
"Adoption Losses: Naturally Occurring or Socially Constructed?" *Child Development*, March/April 2002.

Mary Ann Mason
"Fostering Family," *New Republic*, August 30, 1999.

S. Lynn Mulcare and Herman Aguinis
"Effects of Adoptive Status on Evaluations of Children," *Journal of Social Psychology*, April 1999.

Ellen C. Perrin
"Decades of Research Show No Risk to Adopted Children Raised by Gay Parents," *Insight on the News*, April 22, 2002.

Vidya Rao and Rachel Moody
"Adoption," *British Medical Journal*, October 13, 2001.

| Catherine Siskos and Erin Burt | "The Long Road Home," *Kiplinger's Personal Finance Magazine*, December 2002. |
| Theodore J. Stein | "The Adoption and Safe Families Act: Creating a False Dichotomy Between Parents' and Children's Rights," *Families in Society*, November 2000. |

CHAPTER 4

How Can Families Best Be Supported?

Chapter Preface

According to Matt Cherry and Molleen Matsumura, editors for *Free Inquiry* magazine, "Families are not static, nor is the world around them. . . . Genuine support for families means constantly and flexibly re-examining the relationship between family and society in the lives of free, responsible individuals."

Indeed, the concept of family has changed considerably since the 1960s. The entire Western world has seen social changes such as increasing numbers of women in the workplace and rising divorce rates. One of the most significant changes in family structure is the increase in single parent families. Since 1970, the number of children living in single parent homes doubled. In 1998, 26 percent of all families with children were headed by a single parent. Unfortunately, as single parent families have increased, so too have poverty rates.

The United States has the highest poverty rate of any developed nation. More than 45 percent of single mothers live below the poverty line. The United States also has the highest rate of child poverty in the Western world. In 2000, more than 16 percent of children under eighteen lived below the poverty line, and 37 percent lived in low-income families. The U.S. child poverty rate is two to three times higher than the rates of other industrialized nations. Research suggests that child poverty is linked to poor nutrition and medical care, parental substance abuse, poor academic performance, child abuse, and lower quality child care.

Many of those concerned about child poverty believe that the best way to address the problem is to campaign against unwed childbearing and single motherhood. In 1996, the House of Representatives enacted a series of welfare reform measures that aimed to reduce the number of unwed pregnancies and mothers on welfare. These measures gave states the power to refuse assistance to people under the age of eighteen and ended payments for additional children born to a mother already on welfare.

Some social critics point out that supporters of this type of legislation strive to eliminate the problems associated with single parenthood by stigmatizing unwed pregnancy and single motherhood. According to associate research psychologist Arlene Skolnik, "While not all family restorationists go along with such drastic legislation, they generally use a language of moral failure and cultural decline to account for family change." Skolnik asserts that the United States is the only Western nation to try to reverse the negative effects of single motherhood by calling it immoral. Other developed countries, such as France, the Netherlands, and Great Britain strive to mitigate the effects of single motherhood by providing public assistance, subsidized child care, and paid parental leave from work. As stated by Skolnik, "Most other countries. . .have developed policies in support of working parents, one-parent families, and all families raising children."

Families in the United States have undergone significant changes over the last fifty years. Whether America should address increasing numbers of single parent households by revoking public assistance continues to be fiercely debated. In the following chapter, authors discuss how families can best be supported.

| *"Desperate need on the part of families at all income levels creates a huge market demand for [child] care."*

Improved Day Care Would Benefit the Family

Mona Harrington

In the following viewpoint, Mona Harrington argues that day care is necessary for most families with two working parents. Increased numbers of women in the workplace contributed to women's equality but also weakened the country's child-care system by eliminating the free care that stay-at-home mothers provided. Harrington argues that this free care must be replaced by a national caretaking system that provides quality child care and maintains equality between the sexes. Harrington is a political scientist and the author of *Care and Equality: Inventing a New Family Politics.*

As you read, consider the following questions:

1. According to the author, how was Zoe Baird typical of many professional women?
2. As stated by Harrington, why are women in low-paying jobs worse off in terms of child care than women in high-paying jobs?
3. What are the four premises that the author offers for dealing with the problem of day care?

Mona Harrington, "The Care Equation," *American Prospect*, Vol. 9, July/August 1998, pp. 61–68. Copyright © 1998 by The American Prospect, Inc. Reproduced with permission.

Our family care system is collapsing. When it worked well, it depended on the unpaid labor of women at home. Now that we've lost a great part of that labor force and only marginally replaced it, our society has no new philosophic consensus for an economic system that would support families as care providers. But there is a further element to the problem. As our care system has depended on the unpaid labor of women, it has depended on women's inequality, and it still does, although in new guises.

Maintaining Women's Equality

We need new support systems to enable families to provide good care for their members—on terms of equality for women. Such systems must be deliberately constructed—which means politically constructed. We have to decide as a society about shifts in responsibility for caretaking, shifts in resources, and shifts in costs. And these shifts have to occur in three major sectors of society: in government, in the workplace, and in families themselves.

We do not lack ideas; designs for new care systems are thick on the ground. But we have an ideological block against thinking about such designs in the first place. Deep in American political culture lies a powerful belief in private systems of social organization—belief in the private market as the best means of organizing the economy, belief in the private family as the best means of organizing care and social order. But now most families cannot do all their care work themselves, nor do they have enough money to buy the care they cannot provide. So we are a society without enough care—at all income levels—and we are obviously suffering because of it.

This is where liberals come in. Dealing with the collapsing care system in any realistic way means moving the ideological boundary line between what we consider properly private and properly public business. Moving that line—widening the scope of public responsibility and broadening the going conception of public business—has been the historical role of American liberals. But the problem is that liberals—I mean mainstream liberals in policy-forming, decisionmaking places—are in serious confusion about these issues.

Embracing the idea that women's equal rights should extend into the workplace, liberals have energetically challenged old systems of discrimination. But for women to receive equal treatment, income, status, and authority at work, they have to follow established male employment models—which generally do not take families and care into account. And this is where liberal thinking goes blank. Where do children fit into this picture? Who takes care of them and pays for their care? Conservatives invoke family values, meaning a traditional division of labor in the home. Liberals call for expanding subsidized day care, but they have not squarely confronted the problem conservatives raise of the need for more family time and more parental time with children. Nor have liberals, any more than tradition-bound conservatives, begun to deal seriously with the connections between care and gender equality. The idea of constructing a blend of publicly financed child care, shared parental responsibility, and—crucially—family-focused, equality-focused work time is still in its political infancy.

But the problem is at least on the table. It broke into national consciousness less through deliberate policy initiatives than in a series of public dramas during the first Clinton administration, when liberals whom Clinton brought with him into office confronted the care and equality problem without recognizing its inherent conflicts and explosive potential. Most significant and most confusing was the Zoe Baird affair, the crisis greeting Bill Clinton on the first day of his presidency in 1993.

Mothers in the Cabinet

I can still see Zoe Baird leaning toward the microphone before the Senate Judiciary Committee, eyes puffy, mouth tight, explaining again and again why she had hired illegal aliens as nanny and chauffeur while she worked in the top managerial ranks of the Aetna insurance company, why she had not paid Social Security taxes on them—and why this should not bar her appointment to the office of attorney general.

A lawyer and the mother of a small child, she was in several ways typical of professional women in high-pressure, formerly all-male workplaces. To operate as equals in such environments, these women must put in long, often unpredictable hours. Unless they can rely on housebusbands, who are rare, or nearby at-home relatives, who are almost as rare, they frequently need full-time, live-in help to care for their children. Many, finding their choice of employees limited or relying on personal references for reliable caregivers, turn, as Baird did, to the informal network of undocumented immigrant labor. They thus become lawbreakers—albeit of laws that are so widely broken that they are generally unenforced. Or they can compromise their own work hours on a mommy track—in which case they do not advance along with their male peers, and they do not become candidates for attorney general.

Distribution of Percentage of Earnings Spent on Child Care by Low- and Higher-Earning Families That Pay for Care

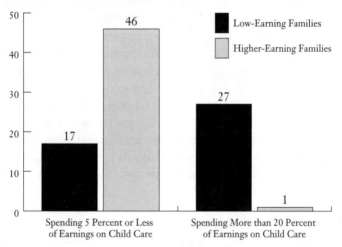

Urban Institute calculations from the 1997 National Survey of America's Families.

President Bill Clinton wanted the attorney general to be a woman; he wanted a Cabinet that "looked like America." With his wife Hillary, he had made a commitment to break the all-male hold on the most senior cabinet jobs—the four power positions. He wanted to be a president known for advancing the equality of women.

Here was the collision of care and equality in the making.

Not all likely women candidates might have fallen afoul of the immigration and Social Security laws, but many would—the top two did, as it turned out. And the country could not have an identified lawbreaker as its top law enforcer.

In part, the Baird crisis occurred because the intricate linkage of care and equality was not politically visible. Even Bill Clinton, the most astute of politicians, didn't see it. He knew of Baird's nanny problem but saw it as a commonplace situation that Baird was in the process of straightening out (she was, at the time, seeking green cards for her employees and paying the back taxes). Senator Joseph Biden, chair of the Senate Judiciary Committee, did anticipate danger. He foresaw a public furor erupting at the news of a lawyer earning $500,000 a year hiring illegal help; it looked like a case of the rich person choosing not to pay decent wages and benefits. That is, he saw class conflict.

What neither man could see, because it wasn't there, was a liberal frame for the problem in front of them. They had no idea that when Zoe Baird walked into the Senate committee room, she carried with her a set of layered and compacted conflicts. They did not grasp that they were watching an increasingly fragile caretaking structure moving toward collapse. They did not see a massive collision occurring between the country's need for caretaking and the standing American promise of equality.

Care and Equality

The movement of women toward equality through paid work was undermining the country's caretaking. But women's continued responsibility for caretaking was, at the same time, undermining their movement toward equality. Statistics tell the familiar story: women's wages lower than men's; women clustered in the lower levels of most workplaces; top corporate management 95 percent male; women in only 10 to 15 percent of the top positions in the professions, most on mommy tracks or in "women's fields"; and even with recent gains, very few women in the Congress or in governorships.

Bill and Hillary Clinton and their enthusiastic backers in women's rights organizations had these statistics in mind in their determination to appoint a significant number of women to the Cabinet and other official positions. But here a plague of confusions surrounding the very concept of women's equality came into play.

The first, set deeply in American history and in mainstream liberal principle, is that there is no unambiguous concept of women's equality, as such. The principle to be honored and protected politically is individual equality, if women were excluded from medical schools, law firms, or police forces, and if political parties were not backing them for stepping-stone offices that led to governorships or to Congress, the principle being offended was individual equality. Women were not being judged on individual merit; they were being judged on the basis of stereotypical ideas about the nature of women as a sex. When women's advocates in the 1960s raised this argument in clear terms, the most egregious barriers to women in the workplace and in public life began to fall. The powerful idea of fairness to the individual was the lever that made the difference. . . .

Impossible Choices

The equality problem goes far beyond professional women like Baird. Most women earning middle-range incomes cannot afford as much support as their families need, and they compensate by racing between job and home to provide as much family care as possible themselves, often working part-time or flex-time. But workers who limit their time on the job, by whatever arrangement, tend to remain at the lower levels of their occupations. And since women are mainly the ones doing this, their choices—which are entirely reasonable and humane—are reinforcing the old pattern of women's work ghettos.

Women in low-wage jobs are worse off, since most simply cannot pay for family care. They often rely on relatives, friends, and neighbors for patchwork care systems that are fragile at best, creating risks of poor care for children and elders, and off-and-on employment records for the women responsible for them. Except where meager public subsidies are available, the frequent result is entrapment of all family members in a downward economic spiral that makes the promise of equal opportunity a cruel joke.

Sadly, care workers themselves generally fall into this last category. Desperate need on the part of families at all income levels creates a huge market demand for care. But as most people who need day or elder care have limited resources to pay for it, caretaking wage levels remain low, and the supply of care workers depends on people who have no choice but to take low-paid jobs. As a result, we are headed toward hardening inequality in the creation of a new, low-wage, servant class that will do our caretaking for us.

Further, as the Zoe Baird story illustrates, a main source of low-wage service labor is immigration—legal and illegal and largely Hispanic. Depending on these workers, we create not just a servant class, but one made up of ethnic minorities who, in large part, do not have the power—and often not even voting rights—to improve their employment conditions politically.

And here is yet another layer of complication in this long story, in a more recent nanny affair—the trial of the au pair Louise Woodward for the death of a baby in her care—the media's stories were filled with controversy about working mothers. In this case, the mother was a doctor with only a part-time practice. Nonetheless, many people blamed her, not the au pair, for the baby's death, reflecting the still-strong conviction that women who can afford to stay home should not be at work in the first place; they should be at home taking care of their families.

Women as Natural Caretakers

Bolstering this belief is the enduring power of the idea that women have a natural capacity for the care of children and others, and that these natural gifts make it right, not simply convenient, for the woman of the family to provide or oversee its care. Whether this idea stems from moral conviction, personal observation, or emotional longing for the securities of a simpler time, it clouds recognition of the fact that most American women are not at home and are not going home— at least on the old terms.

In a final twist, the idea of women's natural caretaking qualities has another powerful effect, which was also at play in the Zoe Baird affair. Some people feel that if women are good at the emotional work of caring for others, they are not good at work that depends on disciplined rationality and toughness—like law.

Missing in this equality-blocking box of stereotypes, however, is the idea that someone who has done caretaking, who understands its demands, who knows its importance, and who recognizes a caretaking crisis when she sees it would be a highly valuable decisionmaker in government or the private sector.

The problem is that as a society we still accept a whole series of connected dichotomies: men/women; tough/soft; reason/emotion; public life/private life. Soft, emotional women are supposed to take care of private life. Tough, rational men are supposed to manage the demanding, dangerous world. In this general picture, concern about care belongs on the feminine, private side of the boundary.

Making care a legitimate public issue, a mixed public-private responsibility, requires dissolving the dichotomies. This is why including women, as women, in public decision-making is important. For one thing, women's presence and visibility in public life weakens the hold of dichotomous thinking. And women have, in fact, furthered this disruption by insisting on putting care high on the public agenda. Former Representative Patricia Schroeder introduced a family and medical leave bill in 1985 and fought for it until it was finally passed in 1993. Child care, health care, and education—the gender gap issues—are consistently pushed by women in Congress, by women governors, by women activists. And women do this not because they are programmed by nature to be concerned about "soft" issues but because they so often have direct personal responsibility for care, which gives them a much-needed perspective on the issue that has been missing from national life.

This is not to say that all women think alike on social issues. Conservative women are as adamant as conservative men in resisting broadened public responsibility for work and family problems and caretaking generally. But that is not a reason for liberals to be squeamish about deliberately adding women's experience to the public debate and making the logic of this position clear. . . .

A New Family Politics

So where do we go from here? Many liberals now are—rightly—calling for new and serious family programs. . . . But we must set about inventing a new liberal family politics based squarely on the twin principles of care and equality. It must be a politics that goes beyond election strategies; it requires a firm, clear philosophy at its base. What follows is a sketch of four premises for such a politics.

Taking care seriously. This means nothing less than asserting a social responsibility for care as a major national value. Liberal arguments have to make clear how tragically mistaken conservatives are to rely on the private market as an adequate distributor of resources for family care. But liberals must also broaden their own conception of the family care crisis—from a focus on low-income families to all families; from a focus on more and better services to the need for more family time as well; from a focus on the responsibility of government to assume more family care costs to the parallel responsibility of corporations and employers to do so. To take these goals seriously means moving beyond rhetoric and marginal programs to large-scale shifts in the use of the country's resources.

Embracing the family. Liberals as protectors of individual rights, which sometimes conflict with family claims, have had difficulty staking out a clear pro-family ground. As a result, conservatives have appropriated the realm of "family values" and have defined these values as individual sexual morality and traditional male/female roles and relations. They also have positioned liberals as corrupters of morality and destroyers of families. Liberals need to contest the conservative position with enthusiastic support for all families—traditional and nontraditional—that provide care for their members.

Adding equality. Equality for women must include equal opportunity, which means significant changes in the economics of caretaking. We need to shift to the society at large a substantial portion of the caretaking costs now carried by unpaid or poorly paid women. For liberals this means the absorption of some costs by employers and taxpayers and an equal division of unpaid labor at home between women and men.

163

Equality also means full participation in the policymaking, rule-making, and decisionmaking that shape the way the society works. Deeply engrained habits and convictions that tend to identify women with private roles and to envision authority as properly masculine stand in the way of this goal. The liberal task is to challenge and dislodge equality-defeating attitudes.

Opening new political channels. A new liberal politics of family care requires a new mode of political thinking. In the face of social trouble, Americans tend to search for abuses of power, enemies, or wrongdoers and devise solutions limited to removing or controlling particular villains (abusive mothers, neglectful fathers, murderous au pairs, and would-be Cabinet members who fail to pay nanny taxes, for example).

To perceive the full range of reasons for our care crisis and to construct new solutions, we need to broaden the scope of public responsibility. We need to enlarge the circle of decisionmaking and debate to include all of the constituencies involved in the care and equality issue: families at all income levels, paid and unpaid caregivers, women in all kinds of workplaces, employers in all kinds of workplaces, teachers, family court judges, health care providers, service workers' unions. We must recognize that our most serious troubles are the work not of removable wrongdoers but of conflicts in interest and imbalances of power that require continuous negotiation.

*"Children are getting less of their parents'
time today than in any previous era."*

Day Care Should Be Discouraged

Karl Zinsmeister

According to Karl Zinsmeister, children fare better when
they are raised by their parents at home instead of by
strangers in day care. He contends that parents and children
need frequent, affectionate contact with each other to maintain strong family bonds. Zinsmeister maintains that parents
should restructure their lives so that their children's needs
come before their own careers and financial goals. Karl
Zinsmeister is the editor-in-chief of the *American Enterprise*,
a national magazine of politics, business, and culture.

As you read, consider the following questions:
1. According to the author, what is one reason that modern
   parents turned to day care?
2. Why does a "carrying system" of child care exist in
   humans, according to Zinsmeister?
3. As stated by the author, how could employers encourage
   parents to spend more time with their families?

Karl Zinsmeister, "Why Encouraging Day Care Is Unwise," *American Enterprise*,
Vol. 9, May/June 1998, pp. 4–8. Copyright © 1998 by American Enterprise
Institute for Public Policy Research. Reproduced with permission.

There is an old saying that goes "Children have a special way of spelling love: T-I-M-E." What the very young hunger for more than for anything else in the world, modern researchers confirm, is closeness with their mothers and fathers.

Unfortunately, children are getting less of their parents' time today than in any previous era. A favorite cartoon of mine suggests how far we've strayed. It shows a corporate type speaking to his secretary from behind a large desk. "I've decided to spend more time with my family," he announces. "See if you can find them."

One professor I know illustrates the problem by way of an analogy. "Let's assume you had some other industry," he says. "The industry made shoes, and then you took a large chunk of the labor force out, something like 40 percent, and you changed nothing much else—you wanted to make the same amount of shoes of the same quality with the same technology. Everybody in the world would think you'd lost your mind. Well, that's basically what we did to parenting."

Leave Child Raising to Professionals

One reason the flight from parenting has been so fast over the last generation is because lots of self-appointed experts have advised the American public that there's no reason not to veer off into other pursuits while leaving the daily raising of children to surrogates. "The care of the young is infinitely better left to trained professionals rather than to harried amateurs with little time nor taste for the education of young minds," insists feminist Kate Millett.

Responsible authorities who ought to have challenged this kind of foolishness mostly failed to do so. One national statement on the family released a few years ago actually defined "parents" as "adult persons who care for children"—making their equivalence to babysitters and day care workers quite explicit. No sensible person actually believes this, of course, but it is becoming our official national orthodoxy anyway, because few people will speak against it for fear of being called the many names that now get slung at someone who defends the natural family. . . .

Over the last decade or two, many discoveries have been

made that help explain why a child's early bonds with his caretakers are so important. Authorities used to believe that babies were essentially passive bundles, unable to perceive or seek out much from their environment. Any social responses were thought to be, as one scientific curriculum put it, "a figment of the over-involved mother's imagination, since baby's behavior is random, uncontrolled, essentially autistic."

Experts asserted that children needed only feeding, protection from danger, and other basic care until they were a year to a year-and-a-half old. And after that, it was said, the young mostly needed discipline and behavioral conditioning. Yale professor Arnold Gesell, the leading child developmentalist of the pre–World War II generation, believed that basic human capacities were biologically programmed into infants, and that they unfolded in stable, predictable ways without much relation to home conditions. Little credence was given to the idea that parents and small babies could have a relationship. Even "as late as the 1960s," Stanford University psychologist Anne Fernald remarks, "some people thought infants were cabbages."

That "expert" view has now been demolished. Against the old assumption that newborns are unable to perceive or seek out much from their environment, researchers have recently demonstrated that babies are sorting and responding to stimuli virtually from birth.

For instance, studies have shown that a one-week-old child will choose his mother's smell over any other. Five-day-olds will turn toward a pad soaked in their mothers' milk, while clean pads produce no response. The journal *Science* has reported that newborns will respond to poems their mothers read out loud before birth, but not to poems previously unheard. In another experiment, one-month-olds became upset when photos of their mothers were accompanied by recordings of someone else speaking. University of Washington psychologist Patricia Kuhl has discovered that six-month-olds can distinguish between their native language and foreign tongues. . . .

So it turns out infants are not cabbages at all. "Detailed studies of the amazing behavioral capacities of the normal neonate have shown that the infant sees, hears, and moves in rhythm to his mother's voice in the first minutes and hours of life," summarize pediatricians Marshall Klaus and John Kennell. "A lot more is happening in infants' minds than we've tended to give them credit for," agrees psychologist Karen Wynn.

Anderson. © 1991 by Kirk Anderson. Reprinted with permission.

All of this confirms the importance of a child's early experiences. It also supports the conclusions of "attachment" researchers like psychiatrist John Bowlby, who hold that babies have powerful internal mechanisms that drive them to connect themselves to their parents. "The bells that the children could hear were inside them," the poet Dylan Thomas once wrote. Apparently the bells that ring within newborns lead them to energetically pursue alliance with their mother, and to become anxious if these efforts are thwarted.

Hunger for their mother isn't something babies can just "get over." It is a need wired deeply into their core. Writer Peggy O'Mara McMahon observes that the mothering behavior of different animal species

> falls into two categories: cache or carry. Species in the cache category are stashed in a den with other offspring while their mothers look for food, do not need to feed often, and do not need frequent physical contact with mother. The species in

the carry category are marsupial-like. Their mothers' breast-milk is low in fat content and must be consumed almost continuously. They are not born in litters, and close physical contact with mother not only ensures frequent feeding, but also stimulates brain development.

From nutritional and other points of view, round-the-clock nursing and a carrying system of child care are not very efficient. So why do they exist in the higher animals? Because frequent suckling provides repeated opportunities for intimate interaction between mother and child—the very sort of contact that encourages higher mental processes in an infant. "Rapid onset of hunger and satiation in the baby," summarizes researcher Blurton Jones, is "a simple mechanism for ensuring that it stays with the mother.". . .

Parental Connections

It isn't only babies who need tight human connections. Parents do too, if they are going to flourish in their role of progenitor. A hint of this was contained in a statement made by PepsiCo President and CEO Brenda Barnes when she resigned her job, to much media comment, a few months ago. "I'm not leaving because my children need more of me," Barnes stated. "I'm leaving because I need more of them."

Many talented women who devote themselves to mothering while their children are young have come to this same conclusion. They do what they do not just out of devotion to their children, but because they have discovered there are deep personal satisfactions awaiting anyone who will pour herself into the role.

A dabbling, partial commitment of mother to child is even harder to sustain than full-blown engagement, notes John Bowlby:

> Enjoyment and close identification of feeling is only possible for either party if the relationship is continuous. . . . Just as the baby needs to feel that he belongs to his mother, the mother needs to feel that she belongs to her child, and it is only when she has the satisfaction of this feeling that it is easy for her to devote herself to him. . . .

A family friend who used daytime babysitters heavily for several weeks when she had to pack for a sudden cross country move told me that the more time she spent away from her young boys, the less adroitness and patience she had for handling them. Likewise, Ohio mother Mary Robin Craig writes of a period when she worked full time and had a nanny that, "On my off days I could see that their lives had a flow that eluded me totally."

It's necessary to get into a swing with children, and simple overlap is a big part of this. There is evidence, as child developmentalist Urie Bronfenbrenner notes, that an infant uses physical, emotional, and probably invisible hormonal tools to "'teach' his parents" how to nurture him. But this can succeed only if the pupil shows up for class.

Day Care in Moderation

Obviously, there will always be families where death, divorce, or poverty make it impossible for parents to be their child's primary caretakers. These families deserve our help, and first crack at the limited number of truly wonderful surrogate caretakers who are able to pour themselves into the nurture of another person's child.

It is also obvious that substitute child care is generally not harmful in small amounts. As psychologist Diane Fisher carefully puts it, "day care can be a place that does not do a great deal of harm to children if they're there for a limited amount." The problem is that rather than just being a filler of gaps, day care is becoming a substitute for parenting in many families.

The question is not whether hired day care should exist (it always will), or whether it should be made as good as possible (of course it should). The question is whether everyday middle-class Americans should produce children without the intention of nurturing them. There is a difference between a compromise made in reaction to some crisis of fate, and an arrangement made simply because one wants to maximize one's own position while ignoring serious costs to others.

By transforming day care from a necessary stopgap for the unlucky few into a normal and accepted part of average lives, we are thoughtlessly taking a step of great consequence. One liberal professional who has devoted her entire working life to overseeing municipal day care programs warns that the shuffling of millions of middle-class children into day care is icy should look like were offered recently by former *New Republic* editor Michael Kelly:

> It would seek to strongly discourage out-of-wedlock births. It would seek to strongly reinforce the idea that it primarily takes not a village but parents—two of them—to raise a child. It would offer help for parents who must work, but it would send an unmistakable message that, whenever possible, it is better that one parent stays home with the kids. The policy put forward by the Clinton administration . . . is irrationally biased toward the form of child care most parents like least—institutionalized group care—and against what most parents want most: to be able to afford to have one parent stay home. . . . Why does the administration seek an economic incentive for parents to choose work over childrearing? . . . If the administration is serious about the best interests of the children, it will correct the anti-home-care bias in its policy.

Not every American child will enjoy the primary energy and devotion of his own parents when he is young—no matter what assistance is offered toward that end. But that ought to be our goal, the ideal toward which all of our encouragements are aimed. It's a simple, practical, and wholesome aspiration.

So what are we waiting for?

| "No group today has fewer rights than
fathers."

Family Courts Harm Fathers and Families

Stephen Baskerville

In the following viewpoint, Stephen Baskerville argues that the family court system is biased against fathers. He contends that family courts deny fathers fair custody and child support arrangements, and he cites examples of men who lost access to their children or had to pay exorbitant court and attorney fees. Baskerville maintains that the family court system allows the government to intrude on the private realm of the family. Baskerville is a professor of political science at Howard University in Washington, D.C.

As you read, consider the following questions:

1. According to the author, how does the plundering of fathers usually begin?
2. How are mothers who abduct their children "rewarded," as stated by the author?
3. According to Baskerville, what is the only way for men to avoid the tyranny of the family court system?

Trevor Gallahan's father is going to jail. He has not been charged with any crime. He is not behind in child support. He has not battered anyone. Yet Ken Gallahan could conceivably remain in jail for the rest of his life. What is his infraction? He does not have $15,000 to pay a lawyer he never hired. He was already jailed indefinitely when he could not pay a psychotherapist he also had not hired and was released only when his mother paid the fees.

Debtors' prisons were theoretically abolished long ago, but this does not stop family court judges from using the bench to shake down fathers who have done nothing wrong and funnel everything they have into the pockets of the court's cronies. In fact the looting and criminalization of fathers like Ken Gallahan is now routine in divorce courts.

Invasive Family Courts

Family courts are the arm of the state that routinely reaches farthest into the private lives of individuals and families, yet they are answerable to virtually no one. By their own assessment, according to Robert W. Page of the New Jersey Family Court, "the power of family court judges is almost unlimited." Others have commented on their vast and intrusive powers less charitably. Malcolm X once called family courts "modern slavery," and former Supreme Court Justice Abe Fortas termed them "kangaroo" courts. One father was told by a judicial investigator in New Jersey, "The provisions of the US Constitution do not apply in domestic relations cases, since they are determined in a court of equity rather than a court of law."

The plunder of fathers invariably begins with the taking of their children. Despite formal legal equality between parents, some 85–90% of custody awards go to mothers. This is despite the fact that it is usually the mother who seeks the divorce, and most often without grounds of wrongdoing by the father. In fact a mother can have a half-dozen previous divorces, she can commit adultery, she can level false charges, she can assault the father, in some cases she can even abuse the children, and none of these (except in extreme cases the last) has any bearing on a custody decision.

A mother who consults a divorce attorney today will be

advised that her best strategy is simply to take the children and their effects and leave without warning. If she has no place to go, she will be told that by accusing the father of sexual or physical abuse (or even simply stating that she is "in fear") she can obtain a restraining order immediately forcing him out of the family home, often without so much as a hearing. She will also learn that not only can she not be punished for either of these actions, they cannot even be used against her in a custody decision. In fact they work so strongly in her favor that failure to apprise a female client of these options may be considered legal malpractice.

Mothers who abduct children and keep them from their fathers are routinely rewarded with immediate "temporary" custody. In fact this is almost never temporary. Once she has custody it cannot be changed without a lengthy and expensive court battle. The sooner and the longer she can establish herself as the sole caretaker the more difficult and costly it is to dislodge her. The more she cuts the children off from the father, alienates them from the father, slings false charges, and delays the proceedings, the more she makes the path of least resistance (and highest earnings) to leave her with sole custody. In short, the more belligerence she displays and the more litigation she creates, the more grateful the courts will be for the business she provides.

The Fatherhood Penalty

For a father the simple fact of his being a father is enough for him to be summoned to court, stripped of all decision-making rights over his children, ordered to stay away from them six days out of seven, and ordered to make child support payments that may amount to two-thirds or more of his income. Like Ken Gallahan, he can also be forced to pay almost any amount to lawyers and psychotherapists and summarily jailed if he is unwilling or unable.

What is happening to fathers in divorce courts is much more serious than unfair gender bias. An iron triangle of lawyers, judges, and women's groups is finding it increasingly easy—and lucrative—to simply throw fathers out of their families with no show of wrongdoing whatever and seize control of their children and everything they have.

Family courts have in effect declared to the mothers of America: If you file for divorce we can take everything your husband has and divide it among ourselves, with the bulk of it going to you. We can take his children, his home, his income, his savings, and his inheritance and reduce him to beggary. And if he raises any objection we can throw him in jail without trial.

Appealing to the Hearts of Women

The real problem is that in America in the year 2000, almost any father, "old" or "new," can find himself a "father without children." What can be done about this? Perhaps, in order to rebuild fatherhood, we need to appeal not to the hearts and minds of men, as sociologist David Blankenhorn and others have suggested, but to the hearts and minds of women. The mother who sabotages the father-child relationship is not always acting out of spite; she may sincerely see little value in this bond; she may want to make a "clean break" and view the father as an intruder—particularly if she wants the children to see the new man in her life as a father figure. In many ways, our culture today encourages such thinking. There have been public service ad campaigns with such slogans as, "They're your kids. Be their dad"; maybe we need one that says, "They're his kids. Let him be their dad."

Cathy Young, *American Spectator*, June 2000.

The astounding fact is that, with the exception of convicted criminals, no group today has fewer rights than fathers. Even accused criminals have the right to due process of law, to know the charges against them, to face their accusers, to a lawyer, and to a trial. A father can be deprived of his children, his home, his savings, his livelihood, his privacy, and his freedom without any of these constitutional protections. And not only a divorced father or an unmarried father: Any father at any time can find himself in court and in jail. Once a man has a child he forfeits his most important constitutional rights.

Keep the State Out of the Home

The words "divorce" and "custody" have become deceptively innocuous-sounding terms. We should remind ourselves that they involve bringing the coercive apparatus of the state—police, courts, and jails—into the home for use against family members. When we recall that those family members may not even be charged with any legal wrongdoing we can begin to grasp the full horror of what is taking place and how far the divorce machinery has been fashioned into an instrument of terror. As citizens of communist Eastern Europe once did, it is now fathers who live in fear of the "knock on the door."

So what can a father do to escape the fate of Ken Gallahan and millions like him? Very little, and divorce manuals encouraging fathers with advice on how to win custody are not doing them any favors. The latest wisdom informs fathers that the game is so rigged that their best hope of keeping their children is not to wait for their day in court but to adopt the techniques of mothers: If you think she is about to snatch, snatch first. "If you do not take action," writes author Robert Seidenberg, "your wife will. If this advice is sound, the custody industry has turned marriage into a "race to the trigger," to adopt the terms of nuclear deterrence replete with the pre-emptive strike: Whoever snatches first survives.

If you don't have the stomach for this, then you probably should not marry and not have children.

"The claim that the courts institutionally are prejudiced against fathers is a canard."

Family Courts Serve Fathers and Mothers Fairly

Tim Tippins

According to Tim Tippins, complaints that the family court system is biased against fathers is based on the fact that mothers are awarded custody of children more frequently than fathers. However, Tippins maintains that custody and alimony arrangements are commonly decided between the divorcing couple, not by a family court judge. Moreover, divorce decrees that exclude fathers are often based on the father's history of abuse or neglect. Tippins concludes that the family court system serves most families fairly. Tim Tippins is the president of MatLaw Systems Corporation, which provides specialized legal information to family-law practitioners.

As you read, consider the following questions:
1. Why is relying on anecdotal evidence to support conclusions about family courts risky, according to Tippins?
2. How does the author define the "tender years presumption"?
3. According to the author, how have support laws hurt mothers?

Tim Tippins, "Q: Are Family Courts Prejudiced Against Fathers? No: Claims of Gender Bias Tend to Come From Men Who Have Gone to Court and Lost," *Insight on the News*, Vol. 17, June 18, 2001, pp. 40–41. Copyright © 2001 by News World Communications, Inc. Reproduced with permission.

There is no shortage of legitimate criticism that fairly can be laid at the doorstep of courthouses across the land, including those courts charged with the extraordinary responsibility of protecting children whose family structure dissolves. Overburdened and under-resourced, the courts do not handle every case with perfection. That is beyond dispute. Like any other profession, lawyers and judges come in all shapes, sizes and levels of competency and rectitude. Some simply are better than others and the quality of the process can be affected by those variables. As long as our system of justice relies upon human engines for its propulsion, it ever will be so.

Yet, for all of the foibles of the U.S. justice system, the claim that the courts institutionally are prejudiced against fathers is a canard. This claim of prejudice, or gender bias, so stridently put forth by fathers' rights advocates, largely is supported by anecdotal evidence, supplied by those disgruntled fathers who were less than happy with the outcome of their cases. They believe that they did not get sufficient access to their children, that they should have won custody or that they were required to pay too much support.

Rather than honestly access their own responsibility for the outcome of their cases, however, these malcontents band together, prop up their most impressive spokesman behind the nearest podium and collectively proclaim to all who will listen, in classic kindergarten fashion, "No Fair," the ultimate refrain of losers the world over.

Anecdotal Evidence Is Unreliable

Reliance upon anecdotal evidence to support any broad conclusions, let alone the kind of sweeping broadside these folks have launched against the legal system is, at best, a risky business. There is no way to determine the accuracy of each individual account or whether it is representative of what occurs across the broader spectrum of cases which are formally adjudicated.

Every horror story can be offset by a countervailing anecdote. For every father with such a story to tell, there is a mother who reposes in her own tormented niche, nurturing her own painful experience, smarting from what she perceives to be an injustice. That is, unfortunately, the nature of any process that concludes with one party prevailing and the other not. Some of these disgruntled litigants are simply more vocal than others. In virtually every instance, the source of the story usually has a personal agenda.

About as close as the fathers' rights advocates get to citing data to support their gender-bias mantra is the fact that mothers ultimately receive custody more often than fathers. From that lone factual nugget, they ask their listeners to leap to the conclusion that this disparity proves that the courts are prejudiced against fathers.

Getting the Facts

It's time for a reality check.

Fact No. 1: Most custody cases find their resolution in a settlement agreement of the parents' own making, rather than in the courtroom. Those that actually are fought through to a judicial decision are, blessedly, the exception rather than the rule. In other words, most of the mothers who have custody attained it with the father's consent, presumably because the father understood and agreed that the best interest of the children was served by such an arrangement.

Fact No. 2: Many of the judges who supposedly are infected with this father-hating virus are themselves fathers. Short of some twisted psychoanalytical theory that only those males seized by self-hatred make it to the bench, this fact might at least give pause to a rational mind in the assessment of the gender-bias claim.

Fact No. 3: Even in the 21st century, when most women work outside the home, practical experience reveals that it still is the mother who bears the lion's share (lioness would perhaps be more accurate) of the parenting responsibilities during the marriage. Many of the fathers who rail the loudest at the unfairness of the system are the same fathers who, while the domestic relationship was intact, couldn't find two hours a week to spend with their children. As soon as litigation begins, however, these same part-time parents act as though they are competing for a "Father of the Year" award.

In contested custody cases, the court typically examines all relevant factors to determine with which parent the children's best interest will most properly be served. One of the factors to which the courts often look is which parent was the primary care-giving parent prior to the onset of legal hostilities. If the children have done well under that parent's care, the courts are understandably loath to disrupt the arrangement, whether the primary caregiver is the mother or the father. Concern for the stability and well-being of the child rightly outweighs the desire of either parent. As the parenting role of fathers slowly has evolved over the last decade or two, as some fathers have become more active in the lives of their children, we already have seen more fathers prevail in custody disputes than was previously the case.

The Child-Support System Serves Fathers Fairly

As president of the National Child Support Enforcement Association, the nonprofit, professional organization representing the child-support community, I have traveled across the country this year and visited many child-support programs in many states. It has been my pleasure to witness, support and advocate in favor of the growing movement toward establishing partnerships between child-support enforcement agencies and community-based organizations to address the needs of fathers. Wherever I am, I continue to make the case that working with fathers, particularly low-income fathers, should be an ongoing part of child support's core mission. My best argument for the child-support system's commitment to working with fathers is that it's a win-win situation for the children and both parents. Children need two parents whether or not those parents live together! Our first guiding principle is that children deserve and need emotional and financial support from both mother and father. Another is that fathers have value to children that goes beyond a dollar amount. Above all, I believe that the child-support program must incorporate what I call the four F's: firmness, fairness, father-friendliness and family focus.

Dian Durham-McLoud, *Insight on the News*, May 1, 2000.

The so-called "tender years presumption" that held that children should be placed with the mother unless she was unfit long has been abandoned. Neither party gets a head start in the judicial race for custody because of legal distinctions based on gender. If our culture further evolves, and more fathers assume a more active parenting role before they have a legal motivation to do so, we likely will see even more fathers gain custody when the domestic relationship is dissolved. Simply stated, we're just not there yet.

Debunking the Gender Bias Myth

The related claim of some fathers—that they are ejected from their children's lives simply because of their gender—is nothing short of ludicrous. The right of the child to have a meaningful relationship with both parents is a core principle within the judicial system. Indeed, where one parent is found to have interfered unreasonably with the child's relationship with the other, courts have been known to switch custody to the other parent, not as a reward to the wronged parent but to preserve the child's right to have a relationship with both parents. Noncustodial parents rarely are limited to supervised visitation, let alone being denied access to their children. Only under egregious circumstances, where a court finds that the child's exposure to a parent would threaten the well-being of the child in some fashion, is visitation restricted to supervised settings or denied. Such limitations usually are predicated on findings by the court, based on evidence, that there has been abuse, neglect or other misconduct.

These same malefactors then clamor from the public stage that they were deprived of their children for no reason other than that they are male, proclaiming to one and all that they are innocent. They had their day in court. They lost, yet some cannot accept the fact that they lost. They wallow in a sea of self-delusion and denial, telling themselves that they played no part in their fate. Far easier to blame the system, and label hard-working judges and lawyers as biased or prejudiced, than to accept responsibility for their own part in it. For every parent, male or female, who is found to have acted so badly as to justify such restrictions, there are tens of thousands more across the land who don't have time to mount the public soapbox—they're too busy enjoying their children and helping them grow to adulthood.

Child Support

Another issue often raised by the gender-bias brigade is child support. They point to the heavy toll that child support takes on their income under the various support guidelines adopted throughout the nation. While many legitimate arguments can be made against the various child-support formulas that have been put in play over the last decade, the fact is that they apply equally to mothers and fathers. Where a mother is the noncustodial parent, her support obligation is determined by the same guidelines as is a father's. If a particular support formula is unfair, it is equally unfair to each, irrespective of gender. The fact that more fathers are on the paying end of these guidelines reflects only that more mothers are custodial parents, which, as outlined above, reflects many factors unrelated to gender-bias.

Indeed, in one respect, the more generous support laws now in force have hurt mothers more than fathers. By heightening the financial consequences that attach to the custody issue, some fathers, who previously would gladly have agreed to allow the mother to assume the burdens of custody, have been motivated to fight for custody or greater custodial time in an effort to avoid or diminish their child-support obligation. Indeed, in New York, for example, the state's highest court intervened to put an end to what it called "visitation by stopwatch" where it was perceived that too many noncustodial parents were fighting for additional access, not for the benefit of their children but to reduce their support obligation.

Child-custody and support laws, and their application in specific cases, are by their very nature at the highest end of the emotional scale in the judicial system. Losing litigants seldom acknowledge that they were the cause of their own demise and the nameless, faceless "system" makes an easy scapegoat. Unfortunately, their impassioned self-delusion is not supported by reality.

"[Covenant marriage helps people] make their marriage choices wisely and deliberately."

Covenant Marriage Would Benefit the Family

John Crouch

In 1997, Louisiana, soon followed by Arizona and Arkansas, became the first state to offer couples a covenant marriage option. Covenant marriage requires couples to undergo premarital counseling and makes divorce more difficult to obtain. In the following viewpoint, John Crouch argues that the high incidence of divorce has weakened many people's trust in the institution of marriage. Covenant marriage, he contends, will strengthen wedding vows and reduce the incidence of divorce. Crouch is an attorney and the executive director for the Americans for Divorce Reform.

As you read, consider the following questions:
1. According to the author, what do his clients dislike about the divorce process?
2. How does the author define the "prisoner's dilemma"?
3. How can premarital counseling strengthen marriages, as stated by the author?

John Crouch, Testimony of John Crouch, Maryland House of Delegates, Judiciary Committee Hearing, March 16, 1999.

I'm a divorce lawyer. I think covenant marriage will be helpful for people who choose it, and for people who don't choose it, and even for some people who don't get married. I think it will reduce fault *and* no-fault divorce. Covenant marriage gives people the freedom to choose a more sustainable kind of marriage, and it gives them guidance from others in the community, to help them make their marriage choices wisely and deliberately.

We divorce lawyers see our clients getting more and more alienated from the system, wanting to take vengeance on each other, and getting the kids involved in their crusades against each other. Our response has been to tell clients: Divorce is a normal part of life. Get some therapy and support groups for yourself and the kids, get over it, and start the whole process over again with someone else. And meanwhile be nice to your ex, and don't use the kids as weapons, even if it means you lose them.

But we have been telling people these things for 30 years, and they just seem to be getting worse, madder, more desperate. So I've been wondering, if divorce is so normal and people have had 30 years to adjust to no-fault, why does it still drive so many people nuts?

Losing Control

One thing that my clients hate about the divorce process is that they are not in control of their own lives. Regardless of who started it, the potential costs of divorce are unlimited. Their lawyer can't even tell them how much it's going to cost—all we can say is that it depends on what the other spouse and their lawyer do. Any divorce can turn out to be a death match where the richer or meaner spouse wins by attrition.

A covenant marriage law would restore some sense of self-control. People who got divorced against their will would no longer feel that they had been totally passive victims whose belief and dedication to the sanctity of marriage had been used against them. They will at least be able to say, "Well, I chose an open-ended marriage." Or, "I brought this on myself by fooling around." Or, "I chose to let him go, and bargained for a viable standard of living for me and the kids."

And for those who choose covenant marriage, it really would give them more control. Many people my age tell me that IF they ever marry, they would want it to be for life. They have seen what it's like to be divorced, they have known parents and children who have little or no contact with one another, and many of them are determined not to live that way. These people's choice to seek a marriage for life is not just romantic, and it certainly isn't from blind love. It's a very sober choice, based on a knowledge of how weak humans are, especially when there are no laws or social conventions to help them live up to their promises. I don't believe these predictions that people will choose covenant marriage lightly, especially with the rigorous counseling that they will be getting. The people who will choose covenant marriage are adults, and we should allow them their choice.

Feeling Secure

People with this legally-protected commitment to their marriage will be more able to prudently invest themselves in the marriage. Today, it hardly makes sense to tie up your whole economic future and emotional well-being in a marriage which has a good chance of not lasting, and people know that.

Similarly, choosing covenant marriage will drastically reduce the incentives that encourage the kind of behavior that leads to divorce. Let's face it—for a lot of people these days, adultery is not a big deal, and after you're married you're still a free agent. You can still look around for someone you like better, who is younger or more successful than your current spouse, and if you decide to switch teams, you just blame it on love, and there's very little social pressure on you to be faithful. Especially when you know your spouse might do likewise at any time. This situation is what economists call "The Prisoner's Dilemma"—an incentive to betray someone who might betray you, even when it's not in either of your interests to do so. Covenant marriage changes the rules on that point back toward what they used to be. The exit doors will no longer be deceptively easy and inviting. It will take two people to decide to end a marriage, plus some marriage counseling. So covenant marriage should not only reduce no-fault divorce, it should reduce fault divorce, too.

Finally, some of the most important beneficiaries of covenant marriage are those who avoid getting into a bad marriage because of it. Pre-marital education has been improved a lot in recent decades. It teaches them skills to communicate and "fight fair" before and during marriage, but it also leads many of them to postpone or cancel their weddings. A lot of it involves interrogations and psychological profiling that will give the couple a lot more information on how they will get along, whether their priorities are compatible, and whether their plans are realistic.

Covenant marriage will give people more self-determination, and along with it, more responsibility. People want more choice and control over their own lives, and they are mature and responsible enough to live with the consequences of their choices. And they will not make these choices in a laissez-faire vacuum: the premarital counseling required by covenant marriage means that others in the community will actively be helping them to take care that their choices are made wisely. I believe covenant marriages will be stronger, on average, than others, and that they will have reduced levels of fault and no-fault divorce.

"[Covenant marriage] perpetuates the myth that divorced people do not honor or value marriage."

Covenant Marriage Would Not Benefit the Family

Ashton Applewhite

In 1997, Louisiana became the first state to offer couples a covenant marriage option, which requires premarital counseling and makes divorce more difficult to obtain. In the following viewpoint, Ashton Applewhite argues that covenant marriage may increase problems within families by making it more difficult to exit a problematic marriage. Moreover, she contends that no-fault divorces, which permit couples to divorce without assigning blame, are sufficiently difficult to deter spouses from heedlessly separating, and stricter marriage laws are not needed. Applewhite is the author of *Cutting Loose: Why Women Who End Their Marriages Do So Well*.

As you read, consider the following questions:
1. On what grounds does covenant marriage permit divorce, as stated by the author?
2. According to the author, what is the sole benefit of covenant marriage legislation?
3. According to Applewhite, idealizing the traditional nuclear family excludes which groups?

Ashton Applewhite, "Q: Would Louisiana's Covenant Marriage Be a Good Idea For America? No: It Won't Lower the Divorce Rate and Will Raise the Human and Economic Cost of Divorce," *Insight on the News*, Vol. 13, October 6, 1997, pp. 24–25. Copyright © 1997 by News World Communications, Inc. Reproduced with permission.

"**C**ovenant marriage," now legally available in Louisiana and pending before numerous other state legislatures, is the first step in a nationwide movement led by conservative Christians and "pro-family" activists to rewrite or repeal no-fault divorce laws. Under covenant marriage, divorce would be permitted only on narrow grounds such as adultery, abuse, abandonment, felony imprisonment or a mutually agreed upon two-year separation. It seeks to "fortify" marriage by making divorce harder and thus less common. It won't work.

Combating the Divorce Rate

The prevalence of divorce in America is a result of sweeping social changes that cannot be wished away with a piece of sanctimonious and punitive legislation. Anticipating litigation, the covenant-marriage contract is really a postnuptial agreement, guaranteeing that those who make mistakes will suffer exceedingly in their undoing, hardly a Christian attitude. If anything, it should be harder to get married, not to end a union gone wrong.

There lies the sole benefit of this legislation: By forcing engaged couples to think a little harder about what they're getting into, covenant marriage should prevent a number of disastrous unions from occurring in the first place. Many more couples, however, pressured into feeling that "marriage lite" is a cop-out, will ignore their misgivings and live to regret it.

Covenant marriage won't affect the divorce rate. Covenant marriage will not succeed in its primary objective because there never has been any correlation between the incidence of divorce and the laws on the books. The surge of divorces in the 1960s well preceded no-fault legislation, for example, and the American divorce rate has in fact declined slightly in recent years. As sociologist Andrew Cherlin of Johns Hopkins University in Baltimore, a noted scholar in the field, puts it, "The great misconception is that divorce laws change people's behavior. People's behavior changes divorce laws." That's why there is no indication that public attitudes support the current backlash.

Many conservatives maintain that if just one spouse can file for divorce, or if the legal hurdles are low, more couples will separate. It's a logical argument, but not an accurate one, because restrictive laws simply are not an effective deterrent. Just as capital punishment does not lower the crime rate and restricting access to abortion only results in more back-alley operations, people who want out of their marriages will find a way—legally if they have the resources, illegally if not. The incidence of desertion and fraud, which does correlate with stricter divorce laws, would increase, as would marital homicides.

Raising the Costs of Divorce

Covenant marriage will raise the human and economic cost of divorce. Because responsibility no longer had to be assigned, no-fault divorce eliminated the need for one spouse to sue the other. This made the whole process more humane, simpler and much less expensive—and is precisely what covenant marriage legislation would undo. Assets would be spent on lawyers instead of building new lives or providing for children, a real irony given the pro-fault movement's "pro-family" stance. Energy would go into excruciating struggles about offspring and property, instead of into figuring out how to maintain decent relations with the person around whom life once centered, and to moving on.

Described in a *New York Times* article, aptly subtitled "Blame is Back," as "an emerging campaign to restore notions of guilt to divorce law," the repeal of no-fault would result in a tragic increase in the kind of hostilities that can turn divorce proceedings into scorched-earth campaigns. As anyone who has been through a "fault" divorce knows, coming up with grounds is the most demoralizing and wounding part of the process. Ruling out mediation or civil compromise, this bitter exercise mires the couple in accusations and repudiations, making it all the harder to heal and move forward. Blame only damages, but the notion of retribution has endless appeal for the self-righteous. Perhaps the blame lobby would find no-fault divorce more palatable if it were renamed "bi-fault."

Covenant marriage will hurt children. Both sides in this debate can cite countless expert opinions as to the effect of divorce on children, whether devastating or benign. Clearly, divorce does not guarantee maladjustment any more than growing up in an intact home guarantees mental health. The real issue is how children of divorce who live in one, or two, calm and happy homes fare compared to those who grow up in intact homes filled with turmoil or icy silence.

One thing all the experts agree on, though, is that witnessing or being party to parental conflict is what harms children. By making their parents' divorce more difficult and more hostile, covenant marriage ensures the prolonged exposure of children to the most damaging possible circumstances: parents who fight. Too often their deliverance is left in the hands of strangers and overburdened courts. Fractured into warring camps, families often never fully recover. Significantly, even psychologist Judith Wallerstein, author of one of the most-cited studies about the negative effects of divorce on children, opposes legal efforts to make divorce harder.

Divorce Is Not Easy

Covenant marriage raises hurdles that already are high enough. The current outcry that divorce has gotten "too easy" is a periodic complaint, recalling Horace Greeley's displeasure in the late 19th century that too many people were getting "unmarried at pleasure." This charge is cheap to make but impossible to substantiate. Everyone believes divorce is a bad thing, yet everyone knows individuals who divorced for good reasons. By the same token, many think divorce is "too easy," but would be hard put to name a single person for whom the process was anything but painful and arduous—as it should be. Fault or no-fault, divorce is not lightly undertaken.

Neither is matrimony, the Donald Trumps of the world notwithstanding. To act as though the Louisiana Legislature, which initiated covenant divorce in 1997, had just invented a way to make marriage binding and meaningful demeans the vows which have joined men and women for millennia.

Covenant marriage is sexist. One of the principal rationales behind covenant marriage is that it will provide wives with legal recourse against errant husbands the way the old laws did. They linked property to "fault," forcing the divorcing wage-earner to continue to support his family and

What Does Covenant Marriage Require?

Covenant marriage is an innovative, optional form of marriage contract that marrying (or already married) couples may choose if they so desire. It became available in Louisiana in August 1997 (Arizona began offering covenant marriage the following year as well). A covenant marriage contract is intended to signify a couple's greater commitment to their marriage, and their voluntary sacrifice of standard access to quick, easy, no-fault divorce in the future. Couples who choose covenant marriage must complete at least a small amount of pre-marital counseling. They must sign and file affidavits attesting to their understanding that marriage is a life-long commitment. And—after divulging to one another all information that might affect the other's decision—they must agree to seek divorce only with approved fault grounds, or after an extended waiting period of two years for no-fault actions. In either case, covenant marriage couples who decide to divorce may do so only after completing required counseling intended to save the marriage if possible.

Katherine Brown Rosier and Scott L. Feld, *Journal of Comparative Family Studies*, Summer 2000.

giving "innocent" wives considerable leverage in negotiating settlements. The loss of this bargaining power concerns women's-rights advocates as well, joining them in an unlikely alliance with "pro-family" forces.

But the automatic assumption that wives are victims does women no favors and is unfair to the many "innocent" husbands whose wives leave them. The underlying notion of innocence vs. guilt should be jettisoned. It reinforces the age-old link between goodness (innocence) and passivity, a big step backward for authentic women's rights. It also completely disregards the fact that divorce is twice as likely to be initiated by the wife as the husband, and that advancements in women's social and political status correlate with access to affordable divorce. Divorce indeed would become less accessible to women under covenant marriage because it would cost so much more.

A Step Back

Covenant marriage ignores social reality. Profoundly reactionary, the covenant-marriage movement invokes a return to a way of life that was rooted in postwar prosperity, only available to a privileged minority and never all that golden. Of course it would be wonderful if everyone lived happily ever after and all children were raised by loving parents who made it home by 3 o'clock. But, like it or not, most parents must work outside the home. Like it or not, the American family is changing shape: 60 percent of families are headed by a single parent, more than half of whom have never been married. Like it or not, marriage is becoming less relevant: about 3.5 million unmarried opposite-sex couples now share living quarters, up from 2 million a decade ago; men and women now marry later, separate from one another more frequently and, once separated, are less likely to remarry.

Because of these and other wide-ranging cultural forces, divorce is here to stay. As sociologist Arlie Hochschild puts it, "Women have gone into the labor force, but . . . , we have not rewired the notion of manhood so that it makes sense to participate at home. Marriage then becomes the shock absorber of those strains." To cope, husbands and wives need help figuring out fairer ways to distribute responsibility and authority. Meanwhile, the question is not whether these changes are good or bad, but how Americans can adapt wisely and compassionately to a domestic landscape in profound transition.

Idealizing the traditional nuclear family excludes not just the divorced, but also widows and widowers, adopted and foster children and all those who love and are loved outside of a legal contract. It sanctions job discrimination against working parents who need all the help they can get. It ignores the fact that divorce often brings terrible problems to light (problems that continue to seethe privately and damagingly in many intact families) and that divorce very often is the right decision for both the adults and the children involved. It denies the reality that many divorced parents continue to cooperate successfully in raising healthy children. And it perpetuates the myth that divorced people do not honor or value marriage. It is time for our religious and political leaders to stop looking back at outmoded models and reach ahead to innovative solutions.

Covenant marriage is morally problematic. Who really believes that physical abuse or abandonment must take place to render a marriage intolerable? Certainly no victim of mental cruelty, verbal abuse, confinement, financial or sexual withholding, threats against children or dozens of other reprehensible behaviors against which covenant marriage will offer no recourse.

Even more troubling is the quality of married life implicitly sanctioned by this legislation. The threat of an ugly, protracted legal battle indeed will immobilize a number of deeply unhappy spouses. But the thought that someone would want to stay married against his or her partner's desires runs contrary to any humane notion of how people who once cared deeply about each other—and may still—should treat each other. What kind of marriage can it be when one spouse is present against his or her will? What kind of life can be lived in rooms full of rage and despair? Wedlock indeed, but no place for children, nor for responsible adults.

"Far from weakening heterosexual marriage, gay marriage would . . . help strengthen it."

Legalizing Same-Sex Marriage Would Strengthen Marriage

Andrew Sullivan

In the following viewpoint, Andrew Sullivan argues that excluding same-sex couples from the right to marry is a violation of homosexuals' civil rights. Furthermore, he contends that same-sex marriage would promote monogamy and stability among all couples, and therefore strengthen the institution of marriage. Sullivan is the former editor of the *New Republic*, a magazine of politics and culture.

As you read, consider the following questions:
1. According to the author, what is the Federal Marriage Amendment?
2. How did heterosexuals change marriage in the 1970s, as stated by Sullivan?
3. Why do conservatives think that gay men threaten the institution of marriage, as related by the author?

Andrew Sullivan, "TRB from Washington: Unveiled," *New Republic*, August 13, 2001, p. 6. Copyright © 2001 by The New Republic, Inc. Reproduced with permission.

In the decade or so in which same-sex marriage has been a matter of public debate, several arguments against it have been abandoned. Some opponents initially claimed marriage was about children and so gays couldn't marry. But courts made the obvious point that childless heterosexuals can marry and so the comparison was moot. Others said a change in the definition of marriage would inexorably lead to legal polygamy. But homosexuals weren't asking for the right to marry anyone. They were asking for the right to marry someone. Still others worried that if one state granted such a right, the entire country would have to accept same-sex marriage. But legal scholars pointed out that marriage has not historically been one of those legal judgments that the "full faith and credit" clause of the U.S. Constitution says must be recognized in every state if they are valid in one state. And if there were any doubt, the Defense of Marriage Act, designed expressly to prohibit such a scenario, was passed by a Republican Congress and President Bill Clinton in 1996.

None of this stopped the Vermont Supreme Court, legislature, and governor from establishing "civil unions," the euphemism for gay marriage in the Ben & Jerry's state. It's been several years since civil unions debuted, and social collapse doesn't seem imminent. Perhaps panicked by this nonevent, the social right in July 2001 launched a Federal Marriage Amendment [which is still being considered], which would bar any state from enacting same-sex marriage, forbid any arrangement designed to give gays equal marriage benefits, and destroy any conceivable claim that conservatives truly believe in states' rights. Even some movement conservatives—most notably The *Washington Times*—demurred. *The Wall Street Journal* ran its only op-ed on the matter in opposition.

Sex and Sexual Difference

Perhaps concerned that their movement is sputtering, the opponents of same-sex marriage have turned to new arguments. Stanley Kurtz, the sharpest and fairest of these critics, summed up the case in August 2001 in *National Review Online*. For Kurtz and other cultural conservatives, the deepest issue is sex and sexual difference. "Marriage," Kurtz argues, "springs directly from the ethos of heterosexual sex.

Once marriage loses its connection to the differences between men and women, it can only start to resemble a glorified and slightly less temporary version of hooking up."

Let's unpack this. Kurtz's premise is that men and women differ in their sexual-emotional makeup. Men want sex more than stability; women want stability more than sex. Heterosexual marriage is therefore some kind of truce in the sex wars. One side gives sex in return for stability; the other provides stability in return for sex. Both sides benefit, children most of all. Since marriage is defined as the way women tame men, once one gender is missing, this taming institution will cease to work. So, in Kurtz's words, a "world of same-sex marriages is a world of no-strings heterosexual hookups and 50 percent divorce rates."

But isn't this backward? Surely the world of no-strings heterosexual hookups and 50 percent divorce rates preceded gay marriage. It was heterosexuals in the 1970s who changed marriage into something more like a partnership between equals, with both partners often working and gender roles less rigid than in the past. All homosexuals are saying, three decades later, is that, under the current definition, there's no reason to exclude us. If you want to return straight marriage to the 1950s, go ahead. But until you do, the exclusion of gays is simply an anomaly—and a denial of basic civil equality.

Homosexuals and Monogamy

The deeper worry is that gay men simply can't hack monogamy and that any weakening of fidelity in the Bill Clinton-Gary Condit [politicians who had extramarital affairs] era is too big a risk to take with a vital social institution. One big problem with this argument is that it completely ignores lesbians. So far in Vermont there have been almost twice as many lesbian civil unions as gay male ones—even though most surveys show that gay men outnumber lesbians about two to one. That means lesbians are up to four times more likely to get married than gay men—unsurprising if you buy Kurtz's understanding of male and female sexuality. So if you accept the premise that women are far more monogamous than men, and that therefore lesbian marriages are more likely to be monogamous than even heterosexual ones, the

net result of lesbian marriage rights is clearly a gain in monogamy, not a loss. For social conservatives, what's not to like?

Changing with the Times

Lesbians and gay men are indisputably a part of the diversity
of this nation. What has made marriage such a durable institution is not its emphasis on conformity, but rather its ability to flex and change to accommodate the purposes for
which it exists. In the 21st century, those goals are different
from what they were 100 or 500 years ago. Marriage no
longer exists for the purpose of forging great dynasties or se-
curing one's lineage or keeping bloodlines clean. Today,
people marry the person they love for companionship and
support. Some marry because they know that raising children and providing them with a secure environment is best
accomplished by a team. These purposes are not contingent
on sexual orientation or gender. They are universal. To serve
these goals, government's singular role should be to help all
who make a commitment along these lines to flourish. That
includes lesbian and gay couples.

Paula L. Ehlebrick, *Insight on the News*, June 19, 2000.

But the conservatives are wrong when it comes to gay
men as well. Gay men—not because they're gay but because
they are men in an all-male subculture—are almost certainly
more sexually active with more partners than most straight
men. (Straight men would be far more promiscuous, I think,
if they could get away with it the way gay guys can.) Many
gay men value this sexual freedom more than the stresses
and strains of monogamous marriage (and I don't blame
them). But this is not true of all gay men. Many actually
yearn for social stability, for anchors for their relationships,
for the family support and financial security that come with
marriage. To deny this is surely to engage in the "soft big-
otry of low expectations." They may be a minority at the
moment. But with legal marriage, their numbers would
surely grow. And they would function as emblems in gay culture of a sexual life linked to stability and love.

So what's the catch? I guess the catch would be if those
gay male couples interpret marriage as something in which
monogamy is optional. But given the enormous step in gay
culture that marriage represents, and given that marriage is

entirely voluntary, I see no reason why gay male marriages shouldn't be at least as monogamous as straight ones. Perhaps those of us in the marriage movement need to stress the link between gay marriage and monogamy more clearly. We need to show how renunciation of sexual freedom in an all-male world can be an even greater statement of commitment than among straights. I don't think this is as big a stretch as it sounds. In Denmark, where de facto gay marriage has existed for some time, the rate of marriage among gays is far lower than among straights, but, perhaps as a result, the gay divorce rate is just over one-fifth that of heterosexuals. And, during the first six years in which gay marriage was legal, scholar Darren Spedale has found, the rate of straight marriages rose 10 percent, and the rate of straight divorces decreased by 12 percent. In the only country where we have real data on the impact of gay marriage, the net result has clearly been a conservative one.

When you think about it, this makes sense. Within gay subculture, marriage would not be taken for granted. It's likely to attract older, more mainstream gay couples, its stabilizing ripples spreading through both the subculture and the wider society. Because such marriages would integrate a long-isolated group of people into the world of love and family, they would also help heal the psychic wounds that scar so many gay people and their families. Far from weakening heterosexual marriage, gay marriage would, I bet, help strengthen it, as the culture of marriage finally embraces all citizens. How sad that some conservatives still cannot see that. How encouraging that, in such a short time, so many others have begun to understand.

"Same-sex partnerships are a . . . step toward the replacement of marriage with a new system of temporary, fluctuating unions."

Legalizing Same-Sex Marriage Would Harm Marriage

David Frum

In 2000, Vermont conferred all the rights and privileges of marriage to homosexual couples by legalizing "civil unions." In the following viewpoint, David Frum argues that the Vermont legislature forced acceptance of gay marriage on the rest of the country. Frum maintains that gay marriage threatens the institution of marriage by changing it from a stable union between a man and a woman to an unstable and temporary agreement between consenting parties. Frum is a columnist for the *National Post*, a contributing editor for the *Weekly Standard*, and the author of *Dead Right*.

As you read, consider the following questions:
1. According to the author, why is Vermont's constitution difficult to alter?
2. What did the 1996 Defense of Marriage Act decree, as stated by the author?
3. According to Frum, why will same-sex unions make children a marketable commodity?

David Frum, "The End of Marriage?" *Weekly Standard*, January 17, 2000, pp. 7–8. Copyright © 2001 by *Weekly Standard*. Reprinted with permission.

W here are they when they're needed, all of our allegedly pro-family politicians? In 2000, the Vermont
supreme court handed down the incredible ruling that marriage violated the state's 1793 constitution. With that decision, the long-simmering theoretical argument over rights
for homosexuals exploded into immediate practical urgency.
Ex-presidential candidates Gary Bauer and Steve Forbes objected, but, so far as we can tell, all of the leading candidates
for president [in the 2000 election] promptly went silent.

The Vermont court ordered the state legislature to confer
on cohabiting homosexuals all the rights and privileges it ex-
tends to married men and women. The court offered the
legislature the option of avoiding the word "marriage"—it
proposed the euphemism "domestic partnership" instead—
but it insisted that whatever names were used, the thing itself had to be the same.

Gay Marriage Is Here to Stay

When Hawaii's supreme court attempted a similarly reckless
adventure in 1996, the state's voters amended their constitution to slap the court down. But Vermont's constitution is
extraordinarily difficult to alter (an amendment must originate in the state senate, requires four separate legislative
votes spaced over four years, must be signed by the governor, and only then goes to the people for their approval) and
so the court's decision is likely to remain law for some time.
Which means, despite the "domestic partnership" alias, that
gay marriage has for the first time been foisted on an American state. For the first time, but not the last. Given the subtle interworkings of the American federal system—and also
given the not-at-all subtle bias of the American legal class
against family and marriage—the Vermont ruling is a clear
and present danger to marriage everywhere in the country.
Even very liberal courts have thus far hesitated to impose
gay marriage on their own states. But Vermont has now offered such courts a means to smuggle gay marriage past their
legislatures and voters, and in a way not easily corrected by
a constitutional amendment.

New Jersey, for example, may be afflicted with the most
liberal judiciary in the country. Its ability to do harm has

been constrained by a state constitution with an effective amending formula. But what happens when a homosexual with a rich Vermont-domiciled partner defaults on a debt in New Jersey? Can the New Jersey courts be trusted to pass up such a glittering opportunity to import gay marriage into their state?

What happens when a Vermont homosexual is hit by a car in Massachusetts, and his partner demands to be recognized as the next-of-kin? Can the Massachusetts courts really be expected to deny this recognition?

Suppose a husband and wife divorce in New York and agree that the wife should have custody of their children. She now moves to Vermont, takes up with a woman, and enters into a partnership. Her husband sues, charging that the wife has created an unsuitable home environment for the children by entering into a non-marital cohabitation. The wife denies that the home is unsuitable: By Vermont standards, she has remarried. Will the New York courts deny it?

The American Family Crisis

The 1996 federal Defense of Marriage Act will quickly prove to be flimsy protection against the potential for legal mischief created by the Vermont court. The Defense of Marriage Act permits the courts and legislatures of the other 49 states to ignore Vermont homosexual partnerships. But it does not prevent courts and legislatures from recognizing such partnerships as marriages if they so choose, and under the pressure of legal conundrums like those above, one or more of the 49 is bound to crack.

In other words, the long-anticipated legal crisis of the American family has arrived, and it has arrived as a nationwide crisis. And yet, the would-be leaders of the nation have shockingly little to say about it. Former Vice President Al Gore issued a brief statement on the day of the ruling applauding the result while clumsily attempting to reassure traditionalists. "I am not for changing the institution of marriage as we have traditionally known it. But I am for legal protections for domestic partnerships." Former presidential candidate Bill Bradley also claims to oppose (or, as his campaign materials cautiously put it, "not support") gay marriage. But he has chosen to duck the Vermont issue altogether. Ditto for Senator John McCain: The otherwise voluble candidate has apparently said not one word about the decision in Vermont. President George W. Bush contented himself with a brief answer to a journalist's question about the case: "I believe marriage is between a man and a woman."

The Slippery Slope

Homosexual couples speak of their loving relationships which couldn't possibly threaten heterosexual families. "Why should society discriminate against our love?" they ask. For that matter, why should society discriminate against any adult relationship? Once gay marriage is instituted, there's no logical reason to deny marriage licenses to any other couple or combination. If a man wants to marry his sister or his Siamese cat or if three or more people want to marry each other, how can society discriminate against their love?

Don Feder, *Insight on the News*, June 19, 2000.

This won't do. Merely stating your support for the law as it existed yesterday does nothing to protect the country from the legal threat it faces today. When the Supreme Court of one of the sovereign states ruled that it could find no "reasonable and just basis" for upholding the constitutionality of the institution of marriage, it posed a legal challenge—and a moral challenge—to the whole nation. This is not the first time that the challenge has been posed: In the series of court cases that challenged Congress's authority to suppress polygamy in the Utah Territory, the federal courts recognized, as Justice Mathews ruled in the 1885 case of *Murphy v. Ramsey*, that "no legislation can be supposed more wholesome and necessary in the founding of a free, self-governing commonwealth, fit to take rank as one of the co-ordinate states of the Union, than that which seeks to establish it on the basis of the idea of the family, as consisting in and springing from the union for life of one man and one woman in the holy estate of matrimony; the sure foundation of all that is stable and noble in our civilization; the best guaranty of that reverent morality which is the source of all beneficent progress in social and political improvement." The federal government cannot and should not exert the same authority over Vermont, a state, as it did over Utah, then still a territory. But if Vermont's revolution is to be contained and corrected, national lawmakers and leaders must articulate their reasons for rejecting it and their plans for mitigating the damage it will do.

Gay Marriage Debases Americans

Advocates of same-sex partnership like to point out that civilizations have experimented with many forms of sexual and family organization. That's true of course—just as it's true that civilizations have experimented with many forms of political and economic organization. What Americans have understood until now, however, is that heterosexual monogamy is the only form of sexual organization consistent with republican self-government. Anything else, as the Supreme Court observed in 1890, tends to "destroy the purity of the marriage relation, to disturb the peace of families, to degrade woman, and to debase man."

The first effects of that debasement are already becoming visible. How often have we heard that the defense of marriage is the moral equivalent of the defense of segregation? Doesn't anybody stop to ponder the horrific trivialization of the evil of segregation implied by this analogy?

But there is plenty more debasement still to come. Same-sex partnerships are a large and decisive step toward the replacement of marriage with a new system of temporary, fluctuating unions that elevate the wishes of adults over the welfare of children. In order to treat same-sex and opposite-sex relationships equally, the new unions will have to be sex-blind: The law will no longer be permitted to take into account the distinctive connections between mothers and children and the special vulnerabilities of women in marriage. Again in order to treat same-sex and opposite-sex unions equally, the new partnerships will have to accept children as a marketable commodity, and to accommodate the alarming new trend toward the purchase and sale of sperm, eggs, and wombs. One of the very first arguments put forward against a federal ban on human cloning was that the ban would threaten the reproductive freedom of homosexuals.

The family is where we learn to be human and to be citizens. Discarding the family in favor of something new will change the meaning of both humanity and citizenship. This is about as large a political issue as there could be. Is it really possible that none of the leading [political figures] is large enough to address it?

Periodical Bibliography

The following articles have been selected to supplement the diverse views presented in this chapter.

Stephen Baskerville	"Nanny State Clobbers Fathers' Rights in Court," *Insight on the News*, June 26, 2000.
Iona Bower	"Family Matters," *Employee Benefits*, March 2001.
Judith Davidoff	"The Fatherhood Industry," *Progressive*, November 1999.
Maggie Gallagher	"Marriage-Saving," *National Review*, November 8, 1999.
Mark Greenberg	"Welfare Reform and Devolution," *Brookings Review*, Summer 2001.
Natasha Lifton	"Child Care Is a Labor Issue," *Social Policy*, Spring 2001.
Ronald B. Mincy	"What About Black Fathers?" *American Prospect*, April 8, 2002.
Walter Olson	"Free to Commit," *Reason*, October 1997.
Theodora Ooms	"Marriage Plus," *American Prospect*, April 8, 2002.
Katha Pollitt	"Shotgun Weddings," *Nation*, February 4, 2002.
Katherine Brown Rosier and Scott L. Feld	"Covenant Marriage: A New Alternative for Traditional Families," *Journal of Comparative Family Studies*, Summer 2000.
Theodore J. Stein	"The Adoption and Safe Families Act: Creating a False Dichotomy Between Parents' and Children's Rights," *Journal of Contemporary Human Services*, November 2000.
David Thomson	"How History Is Failing Our Families," *Family Matters*, Autumn 1999.
Garland Waller	"Biased Family Court System Hurts Mothers," *Off Our Backs*, November 2001.
Cathy Young	"The Sadness of the American Father," *American Spectator*, June 2000.
Martha J. Zaslow and Kathryn Tout	"Child Care Quality Matters," *American Prospect*, April 8, 2002.

For Further Discussion

Chapter 1

1. Barbara LeBey outlines four factors that contributed to the decline of the traditional family: the sexual revolution, women's liberation, divorce, and increased mobility. David Blankenhorn argues that the decline in nuclear families is abating. Considering each author's argument, do you think that modern families will revert to a traditional structure after decades of modernization? Explain your answer using specifics from both viewpoints and your own personal observations.

2. Maggie Gallagher argues that parents should avoid divorce at all costs because of the damaging effect divorce has on children. Suzanne Moore contends that divorce, per se, is not harmful, but rather it is contentious divorce resulting in estrangement of one or both parents from their children that is damaging. With whose argument do you most agree? Explain your answer.

3. According to Richard Lowry, stay-at-home mothers provide better care for their children than mothers who work. On the contrary, Reed Karaim maintains that working mothers teach their children useful life skills, such as independence, hard work, and ambition. Based on your own experience, do you think stay-at-home or working mothers are better caretakers of their children? Explain.

Chapter 2

1. Linda J. Waite argues that marriage confers benefits on couples and their children that other unions do not. Dorian Solot maintains that families headed by unmarried couples can be as healthy as families headed by married couples. Compare the opinions presented in the two viewpoints and then formulate your own assessment of whether marriage is necessary to healthy families.

2. Alan W. Dowd contends that fathers are essential to children's health. Louise B. Silverstein and Carl F. Auerbach maintain that children benefit from any stable, supportive parent, regardless of gender. Whose argument do you find most convincing? Explain your answer.

3. Steven E. Rhoads argues that men and women are biologically programmed to enact traditional gender roles in marriage. Steven L. Nock asserts that male and female roles in marriage need to keep up with changing social trends that afford women more equality. Considering each author's evidence, do you think that men and women should adhere to certain roles in relationships? Why, or why not?

Chapter 3

1. Elizabeth Bartholet argues that placing troubled children in permanent adoptive homes as quickly as possible is preferable to returning them to abusive biological parents or foster care. Evelyn Burns Robinson contends that adoption should be avoided because it is a permanent solution to temporary problems. With whose argument do you most agree? Citing from both texts, explain why you think adoption should be encouraged or discouraged.

2. According to Albert R. Hunt, children raised by gay and lesbian couples fare as well as children raised by heterosexual couples. Paul Cameron argues that gay-rights activists misinterpret statistics to further their own agenda. Whose evidence do you find most convincing and why?

Chapter 4

1. Mona Harrington argues that most families need full-time day care to allow both parents to pursue their career goals. Karl Zinsmeister maintains that parents should rethink their professional aspirations if their jobs take them away from their children. Whose argument do you find most persuasive? That is, do you think that government should help improve day care or provide assistance to families that have one stay-at-home parent? Explain, using specifics from both texts.

2. According to Stephen Baskerville, "with the exception of convicted criminals, no group today has fewer rights than fathers." However, Tim Tippins argues that fathers who complain about the family court system infringing on their rights cannot accept that their own actions contributed to the court decisions. With whose opinion do you most agree? Explain.

3. John Crouch contends that covenant marriage would strengthen marital bonds and reduce divorce. Ashton Applewhite argues that covenant marriage would not undo the social changes that led to a decline in marriage and high incidence of divorce. Citing from both authors, explain why you think covenant marriage would succeed or fail in its effort to fortify marriage.

4. According to Andrew Sullivan, same-sex marriage would reinforce the institution of marriage by promoting stability and monogamy. David Frum argues that same-sex marriages would threaten the institution of marriage by promoting instability. Do you think that same-sex marriage threatens heterosexual marriage? Why or why not?

Organizations to Contact

The editors have compiled the following list of organizations concerned with the issues debated in this book. The descriptions are derived from materials provided by the organizations. All have publications or information available for interested readers. The list was compiled on the date of publication of the present volume; names, addresses, phone and fax numbers, and e-mail and Internet addresses may change. Be aware that many organizations take several weeks or longer to respond to inquiries, so allow as much time as possible.

Adoptive Families of America (AFA)
333 Highway 100 N., Minneapolis, MN 55422
(612) 535-4829 • fax: (612) 535-7808
e-mail: llynch@uslink.net • website: www.adoptivefam.org

AFA serves as an umbrella organization supporting adoptive parents groups. It provides problem-solving assistance and information about the challenges of adoption to members of adoptive and prospective adoptive families. It also seeks to create opportunities for successful adoptive placement and supports the health and welfare of children without permanent homes. AFA publishes the *Guide to Adoption* once a year and the bimonthly magazine *Adoptive Families* (formerly *Ours* magazine).

American Family Communiversity (AFCO)
542 N. Artesian St., Chicago, IL 60612
(312) 738-2207 • fax: (312) 738-2207

AFCO is a multidisciplinary action and education agency engaged in upgrading the various policies, practices, procedures, professions, systems, and institutions affecting the stability and viability of marriage. It publishes the books *Divorce for the Unbroken Marriage* and *Therapeutic Family Law* as well as several monographs.

American Life League (ALL)
PO Box 1350, Stafford, VA 22555
(540) 659-4171 • fax: (540) 659-2586
e-mail: jbrown@all.org • website: www.all.org

ALL is a pro-life organization that provides books, pamphlets, and other educational materials to organizations opposed to abortion, euthanasia, and physician-assisted suicide. It publishes booklets, reports, and pamphlets such as *How the I.U.D. and "The Pill" Work*, *Gambling with Life*, *Contraception and Abortion*, *The Deadly Connec-*

tion, What Is RU-486? and *What Is Norplant?* as well as the bimonthly magazine *Celebrating Life.*

American Public Human Services Association (APHSA)
810 1st St. NE, Suite 500, Washington, DC 20002
(202) 682-0100 • fax: (202) 289-6555
e-mail: jpatterson@aphsa.org • website: www.aphsa.org
APHSA is an organization of members of human services agencies and other individuals interested in human service issues. The association's mission is to develop, promote, and implement public human services policies that improve the health and well-being of families, children, and adults. Their publications include the professional journal *Policy & Practice* and the annual *Public Human Services Directory.*

Child Care Action Campaign (CCAC)
330 7th Ave., 17th Floor, New York, NY 10001
(212) 239-0138 • fax: (212) 268-6515
e-mail: info@childcareaction.org
website: www.childcareaction.org
CCAC is a group of individuals and organizations interested and active in child care. Its purposes are to alert the country to the problems of and need for child care services, analyze existing services and identify gaps, prepare and disseminate information gathered through inquiries, work directly with communities to stimulate the development of local task forces, and bring pressing legislative action or inaction to public attention. CCAC publishes several books, including *An Employer's Guide to Child Care Consultants* and the bimonthly newsletter *The Child Care ActioNews* as well as several resource guides for parents.

Children of Lesbians and Gays Everywhere (COLAGE)
3543 18th St., Suite 1, San Francisco, CA 94110
(415) 861-5437 • fax: (415) 255-8345
e-mail: collage@colage.org • website: www.colage.org
COLAGE is a national and international organization that supports young people with lesbian, gay, bisexual, and transgender (LGBT) parents. Their mission is to foster the growth of daughters and sons of LGBT parents by providing education, support, and community. Their publications include such newsletters as *Tips for Making Classrooms Safer for Students with LGBT Parents* and *COLAGE Summary.*

Child Welfare League of America (CWLA)
440 1st St. NW, 3rd Floor, Washington, DC 20001
(202) 638-2952 • fax: (202) 638-4004
e-mail: info@cwla.org • website: www.cwla.org

The CWLA, a social welfare organization concerned with setting standards for welfare and human services agencies, works to improve care and services for abused, dependent, or neglected children, youth, and their families. It provides consultation and conducts research on all aspects of adoption. It publishes the bimonthly journal *Child Welfare* as well as several books, including *Child Welfare: A Journal of Policy, Practice, and Program.*

Coalition on Human Needs (CHN)
1120 Connecticut Ave. NW, Suite 910, Washington, DC 20036
(202) 223-2532 • fax: (202) 223-2538
e-mail: chn@chn.org • website: www.chn.org

The coalition is an advocacy organization concerned with such issues as education, federal budget and tax policy, health care, housing, and public assistance. It lobbies for adequate federal funding for welfare, Medicaid, and other social services. CHN's publications include *How the Poor Would Remedy Poverty* and the bimonthly newsletter *Insight/Action.*

Concerned Women for America (CWFA)
1015 15th St. NW, Suite 1100, Washington, DC 20005
(202) 488-7000 • fax: (202) 488-0806
e-mail: mail@cwfa.org • website: www.cwfa.org

The CWFA is an educational and legal defense foundation that seeks to strengthen the traditional family by promoting Judeo-Christian moral standards. It opposes gay marriage and the granting of additional civil rights protections to gays and lesbians. The CWFA publishes the monthly magazine *Family Voice* and various position papers on gay marriage and other issues.

Families and Work Institute (FWI)
267 5th Ave., 2nd Floor, New York, NY 10016
(212) 465-2044 • fax: (212) 465-8637
e-mail: dmoore@familiesandwork.org
website: www.familiesandwork.org

The institute addresses the changing nature of work and family life by fostering mutually supportive connections among workplaces, families, and communities. It publishes research reports and other information under the headings General Work-Family Issues, Dependent Care Issues, Leave Issues, and International Work-Family Issues.

Family Research Council (FRC)
801 G St. NW, Washington, DC 20001
(202) 393-2100 • fax: (202) 393-2134
website: www.frc.org

The council is a research, resource, and educational organization that promotes the traditional family, which the council defines as a group of people bound by marriage, blood, or adoption. It opposes gay marriage, adoption rights for homosexual couples, and no-fault divorce. The FRC publishes numerous reports with conservative perspectives on issues affecting the family, including "Free to Be Family" as well as the monthly newsletter *Washington Watch* and the bimonthly journal *Family Policy.*

Family Research Institute (FRI)
PO Box 62640, Colorado Springs, CO 80962-0640
(303) 681-3113
website: www.familyresearchinst.org

The FRI distributes information about family, sexuality, and substance abuse issues. It believes that strengthening marriage would reduce many social problems, including crime, poverty, and sexually transmitted diseases. The institute publishes the bimonthly newsletter *Family Research Report* as well as the position paper "What's Wrong with Gay Marriage?"

Family Service Canada
404-383 Parkdale Ave., Ottawa, ON K1Y 4R4
(613) 722-9006 • (800) 668-7808
fax: (613) 722-8610
e-mail: info@familyservicecanada.org
website: www.familyservicecanada.org

Family Service Canada is a nonprofit, national organization that represents the concerns of families and family-serving agencies across Canada. The organization's mission is to promote families as the primary source of nurture and development of individuals, to promote quality services that strengthen families and communities, and to advocate policies and legislation that advance family well-being in Canada. The organization's publications include the quarterly newsletter *Let's Talk Families* and numerous documents, such as *When Parents Separate or Divorce: Helping Your Child Cope* and *Coping with Tricky Times: Conflict Resolution in Adult/Child Relationships.*

Focus on the Family
8605 Explorer Dr., Colorado Springs, CO 80920
(800) 232-6459 • fax: (719) 548-4525
website: www.family.org

Focus on the Family is a conservative Christian organization that promotes traditional family values and gender roles. Its publications include the monthly magazine *Focus on the Family* and the reports "Setting the Record Straight: What Research Really Says About the Social Consequences of Homosexuality," "No-Fault Fallout: The Grim Aftermath of Modern Divorce Law and How to Change It," "Only a Piece of Paper? The Unquestionable Benefits of Lifelong Marriage," and "'Only a Piece of Paper?' The Social Significance of the Marriage License and the Negative Consequences of Cohabitation."

Lambda Legal Defense Fund
120 Wall St., Suite 1500, New York, NY 10005
(212) 809-8585 • fax: (212) 809-0055
website: www.lambdalegal.org

Lambda is a public-interest law firm committed to achieving full recognition of the civil rights of lesbians, gay men, and people with HIV/AIDS. The firm addresses a variety of issues, including equal marriage rights, parenting and relationship issues, and domestic-partner benefits. It believes marriage is a basic right and an individual choice. Lambda publishes the quarterly *Lambda Update*, the pamphlet *Freedom to Marry*, and several position papers on same-sex marriage.

National Coalition to End Racism in America's Child Care System
22075 Koths Ave., Taylor, MI 48180
(313) 295-0257

The coalition's goal is to ensure that all children requiring placement outside the home, whether through foster care or adoption, are placed in the earliest available home most qualified to meet the child's needs. It promotes the view that children in foster care should not be moved after initial placement just to match them with foster parents of their own race. The coalition publishes the *Children's Voice* quarterly.

National Council on Family Relations (NCFR)
3989 Central Ave. NE, Suite 550, Minneapolis, MN 55421
(612) 781-9331 • fax: (763) 781-9348
e-mail: info@ncfr.com • website: www.ncfr.com

The council is made up of social workers, clergy, counselors, psychologists, and others who research issues relating to the family in such fields as education, social work, psychology, sociology, home economics, anthropology, and health care. It provides counseling through its Certified Family Life Educators Department. The NCFR publishes several books, audio- and videotapes, and the quarterlies *Journal of Marriage* and the *Family and Family Relations.*

Reunite, Inc.
PO Box 694, Reynoldsburg, OH 43068
(614) 861-2584 • fax: (614) 861-2584

The organization's objectives are to educate the public on the need for adoption reform, encourage legislative changes, and assist in adoptee, adoptive parent, and birth parent searches when all parties have reached majority. It publishes a brochure, *Reunite.*

Single Parent Resource Center
141 W. 28th St., Suite 302, New York, NY 10001
(212) 951-7030
website: www.singleparentsusa.com

The center's goal is to provide single parents with the resources to lead normal family lives and to establish a network of local single-parent groups so that such groups will have a collective political voice. It distributes "Kid-Paks," "Parent-Paks," and the "Tips for Safety" video kits by order form.

Bibliography of Books

Anne-Marie Ambert — *The Effect of Children on Parents.* Binghamton, NY: Haworth, 2001.

Julie Ann Barnhill — *Til Debt Do Us Part: Marriage, Money, and How to Talk About It.* Phoenix: Harvest House, 2002.

Jonetta Rose Barras — *Whatever Happened to Daddy's Little Girl? The Impact of Fatherlessness on Black Women.* New York: Ballantine, 2002.

William J. Bennett — *The Broken Hearth: Reversing the Moral Collapse of the American Family.* New York: Doubleday, 2002.

Kate Bingham — *Cohabitation.* Chester Springs, PA: Dufour, 1998.

Thomas E. Buckley — *The Great Catastrophe of My Life: Divorce in the Old Dominion.* Chapel Hill: University of North Carolina Press, 2002.

Lynne M. Casper and Suzanne M. Bianchi — *Continuity and Change in the American Family.* Thousand Oaks, CA: Sage, 2001.

Roberta Chad — *When Staying Home Is Not an Option: A Working Mother's Guide to Creative Time with the Young Ones.* Bedminster, NJ: Achievers Technology Resource, 2002.

Ava Chin — *Split: Stories from a Generation Raised on Divorce.* New York: Contemporary, 2002.

William J. Doherty and Barbara Z. Carlson — *Putting Family First: Successful Strategies for Reclaiming Family Life in a Hurry Up World.* New York: Owl, 2002.

Guy Duty — *Divorce and Remarriage.* Minneapolis: Bethany House, 2002.

Anne Taylor Fleming — *Marriage: A Duet.* Sunnyvale, CA: Hyperion, 2003.

Deborah F. Glazer and Jack Drescher — *Gay and Lesbian Parenting.* Binghamton, NY: Haworth, 2001.

Al Gore and Tipper Gore — *Joined at the Heart: The Transformation of the American Family.* New York: Henry Holt, 2002.

Betsy McAllister Groves — *Children Who See Too Much: Lessons from the Child Witness to Violence Project.* Boston: Beacon, 2003.

Angela Hayden — *Dead Wrong: The Truth About Domestic Violence, Incest, and Child Abuse.* Washington, DC: PublishAmerica, 2002.

Barbara Hobson	*Making Men into Fathers: Men, Masculinities, and the Social Politics of Fatherhood.* Cambridge, MA: Cambridge University Press, 2002.
Susan E. Horner and Kelly Fordyce Martindale	*Loved By Choice: True Stories That Celebrate Adoption.* Grand Rapids, MI: Fleming H. Revell, 2002.
Noelle Howey et al.	*Out of the Ordinary: Essays on Growing Up with Gay, Lesbian, and Transgender Parents.* New York: St. Martin's, 2000.
Karen Ivano	*Adoption: The Birth of a Real Mom, My Journal.* Philadelphia: Xlibris, 2002.
John F. Kippley and Sheila K. Kippley	*The Art of Natural Family Planning.* Cincinnati: Couple to Couple League, 1997.
John E. LaMuth	*A Revolution in Family Values: Spirituality for a New Millennium.* Lucerne Valley, CA: Fairhaven, 2001.
Barbara LeBey	*Family Estrangements: How They Begin, How to Mend Them, How to Cope with Them.* Atlanta: Longstreet, 2001.
Valerie Lehr	*Queer Family Values: Debunking the Myth of the Nuclear Family (Queer Politics, Queer Theories).* Philadelphia: Temple University Press, 1999.
Martha Manning	*The Common Thread: Mothers, Daughters, and the Power of Empathy.* New York: William Morrow, 2002.
Patricia Morgan	*Marriage Lite: The Rise of Cohabitation and Its Consequences.* London: Institute for the Study of Civil Society, 2000.
Jon Morris	*Road to Fatherhood: How to Help Young Dads Become Loving and Responsible Parents.* Buena Park, CA: Morning Glory, 2002.
Rosemary Radford Ruether	*Christianity and the Making of the Modern Family: Ruling Ideologies, Diverse Realities.* Boston: Beacon, 2001.
Rita James Simon and Howard Altstein	*Adoption, Race, and Identity: From Infancy to Young Adulthood.* Somerset, NJ: Transaction, 2002.
Karen Struening	*New Family Values: Liberty, Equality, Diversity.* Lanham, MD: Rowman & Littlefield, 2002.
Julie M. Thompson	*Mommy Queerest: Contemporary Rhetorics of Lesbian Maternal Identity.* Amherst: University of Massachusetts Press, 2002.
Marvin D. Todd and John Kohls	*Linked for Life: How Our Siblings Affect Our Lives.* Sacramento: Citadel, 2001.

Sam Torode,
Bethany Torode,
and J. Budziszewski

Open Embrace: A Protestant Couple Rethinks Contraception. Grand Rapids, MI: William B. Eerdman's, 2002.

Linda J. Waite and
Maggie Gallagher

The Case for Marriage: Why Married People Are Happier, Healthier, and Better Off Financially. New York: Doubleday, 2000.

Leaford C. Williams

Boys Without Dads: When Dads Abandon Homes. North Carolina: Professional, 2002.

Susan Wisdom and
Jennifer Green

Stepcoupling: Creating and Sustaining a Strong Marriage in Today's Blended Family. Three Rivers, MI: Three Rivers, 2002.

Index